OVERTURE O

in associa

E

We are delighted to have the opportunity to work with Overture Publishing on this new series of opera guides and to build on the work English National Opera did over twenty years ago on the Calder Opera Guide Series. As well as reworking and updating existing titles, Overture and ENO have commissioned new titles for the series and all of the guides will be published to coincide with repertoire being staged by the company at the London Coliseum.

Idomeneo is our first entirely new commission in the series, following an updated reissue of *Tosca*. It marks the opening in June 2010 of a new production of Mozart's first mature masterpiece, directed by Katie Mitchell and conducted by ENO's award-winning Music Director Edward Gardner. The cast features some of Britain's outstanding Mozartian singers, including Paul Nilon, Robert Murray, Sarah Tynan and Emma Bell.

We hope that these guides will prove an invaluable resource now and for years to come, and that by delving deeper into the history of an opera, the poetry of the libretto and the nuances of the score, readers understanding and appreciation of the opera and the art form in general will be enhanced.

John Berry
Artistic Director, ENO
June 2010

The publisher John Calder began the Opera Guides series under the editorship of the late Nicholas John in association with English National Opera in 1980. It ran until 1994 and eventually included forty-eight titles, covering fifty-eight operas. The books in the series were intended to be companions to the works that make up the core of the operatic repertory. They contained articles, illustrations, musical examples and a complete libretto and singing translation of each opera in the series, as well as bibliographies and discographies.

The aim of the present relaunched series is to make available again the guides already published in a redesigned format with new illustrations, updated reference sections and a literal translation of the libretto that will enable the reader to get closer to the meaning of the original. New guides of operas not already covered will be published alongside the redesigned ones from the old series.

Gary Kahn
Series Editor

Idomeneo

Wolfgang Amadeus Mozart

Overture Opera Guides
Series Editor
Gary Kahn

Editorial Consultant
Philip Reed
Head of Publications, ENO

OVERTURE

OVERTURE OPERA GUIDES
in association with

EN
O

Overture Publishing
an imprint of

ONEWORLD CLASSICS
London House
243-253 Lower Mortlake Road
Richmond
Surrey TW9 2LL
United Kingdom

This *Idomeneo* Opera Guide first published by Overture Publishing,
an imprint of Oneworld Classics Ltd, 2010

Translation © Charles Johnston, 2010
Reproduced by kind permission of Harmonia Mundi

Extracts from Mozart's letters reproduced by kind permission of Penguin
Books Ltd from *Mozart: A Life in Letters* (Penguin Classics, 2006)

Cover image: culture-images/Lebrecht Music & Arts

Printed in United Kingdom by TJ International, Padstow, Cornwall

ISBN: 978-1-84749-539-6

Contents

List of Illustrations

1. Wolfgang Amadeus Mozart.
Detail from a family portrait painted in late 1780 or early 1781,
around the time of the composition of *Idomeneo*.

2. Title page of the libretto for the first performance (top left); 3. Anton Raaf, the first Idomeneo (top right); 4. Interior of the Cuvilliés-Theater, Munich, where *Idomeneo* had its premiere (below).

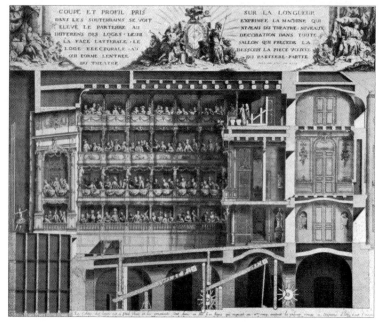

5. The 1951 production directed by Carl Ebert at the Glyndebourne Festival that began the *Idomeneo* revival. Alexander Young as High Priest, Sena Jurinac as Ilia, Richard Lewis as Idomeneo, Léopold Simoneau as Idamante, Alfred Poell as Arbace and Birgit Nilsson as Elettra in Oliver Messel's designs.

Two productions in neo-classical style from the 1960s:
6. Maggio Musicale, Florence in 1962 (above);
7. Benjamin Britten's English Opera Group in 1969 (below).

8. Luciano Pavarotti as Idomeneo and Gundula Janowitz as Ilia in the Carl Ebert Glyndebourne production in 1964 (above). 9. The Sadler's Wells Opera production directed by Glen Byam Shaw and designed by Motley at the London Coliseum in 1970. Anne Evans as Ilia, Hugh Beresford as High Priest and Josephine Barstow as Idamante (below).

10. The first Royal Opera House production, in 1978,
directed by Götz Friedrich and designed by Stefanos Lazaridis.
Magdalena Cononovici as Elettra, Janet Baker as Idamante
and Stuart Burrows as Idomeneo.

11. One of the first deconstructed productions:
Uta Priew as Idamante and Magdalena Hajossyová as Elettra,
directed by Ruth Berghaus and designed by Peter Sykora
at the Staatsoper Berlin in 1981.

12. The much-travelled production directed
and designed by Jean-Pierre Ponnelle at the Lyric Opera
of Chicago in 1977. Christiane Eda-Pierre as Ilia
and Maria Ewing as Idamante.

Four Idomeneos in the Ponnelle production at the Met:
13. Luciano Pavarotti in 1982 (top left). 14. Anthony Rolfe Johnson in 1994
(top right); 15. Plácido Domingo in 1994 (bottom left);
16. Ben Heppner in 2006 (bottom right).

17. The Glyndebourne production directed by Trevor Nunn and designed by John Napier in 1983. Carol Vaness as Elettra, Philip Langridge as Idomeneo, Jerry Hadley as Idamante and Margaret Marshall as Ilia (above). 18. John Copley's 1989 San Francisco production, designed by John Conklin. Hans Peter Blochwitz as Idamante and Karita Mattila as Ilia standing behind the kneeling Wiesław Ochman as Idomeneo (below).

19. The final scene of Act Three in Johannes Schaaf's 1989 Royal Opera House production, designed by Hans Schavernoch. Ann Murray on the left as Idamante and Sylvia McNair on the right as Ilia being held aloft for their coronation (above). 20. Harry Kupfer's 1990 production for the Komische Oper Berlin, designed by Reinhart Zimmermann. Günter Neumann as Idomeneo (below).

21. Frank Corsaro directed and Maurice Sendak designed the opera for Los Angeles Music Center Opera in 1990 to emphasize its autobiographical elements. Susan Quittmeyer as Idamante and Siegfried Jerusalem as Idomeneo (above).

22. Peter Mussbach's production, designed by Nina Ritter, at the Holland Festival in 1991. Laurence Dale as Idamante in the foreground, with John David de Haan as Arbace and Ben Heppner as Idomeneo at the rear (below).

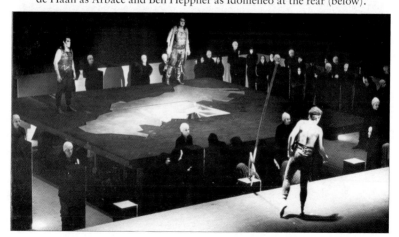

23. David McVicar's production for Flanders Opera,
designed by Michael Vale, first seen in 1999. Guy de Mey
in red as High Priest in the 2003 revival.

24. Janis Kelly as Elettra in the Opera North production directed by Tim Albery and designed by Dany Lyne in 2003 (above). 25. Magdalena Kožená as Idamante in the set designed by Anish Kapoor for the Peter Sellars production at Glyndebourne in 2003 (below).

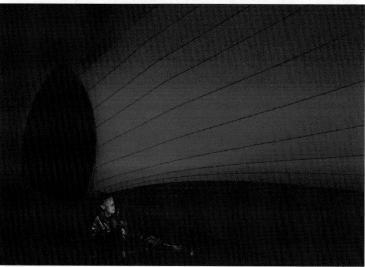

26. Graham Vick's *King Idomeneo* for Birmingham Opera Company, designed by Stuart Nunn, in 2008. It was performed with a group of amateur local performers alongside the professional singers.

27. *Idomeneo* at the restored Cuvilliés-Theater, Munich,
in June 2008. It was directed by Dieter Dorn and designed by
Jürgen Rose. John Mark Ainsley as Idomeneo.

Idomeneo and the Background
of the Enlightenment

Nicholas Till

Idomeneo is a hybrid work of uncertain genre: supposedly an Italian *opera seria*, it is in fact much more closely related to French *tragédie lyrique*, to which Mozart turned for his libretto for the opera. Whereas Metastasian *opera seria* typically took subjects from classical history rather than myth and eschewed grand scenic effects, French opera drew on classical mythology and incorporated the attributes of what critics called the *merveilleux*, including supernatural effects and divine interventions. Unlike *opera seria*, *tragédie lyrique* also included dance and important parts for chorus, both of which are present in *Idomeneo* (although the concluding ballet is usually omitted in performance today). The fact that *Idomeneo* is a French opera in all but name and language gave Mozart the opportunity to work on monumental scenes of high drama which included a storm, a shipwreck, a sea monster and an oracular voice. The outcome is that *Idomeneo* is the most imposing work that he ever wrote.

The hybridity of *Idomeneo*'s genre reflects Mozart's own sense of cultural uncertainty when he was writing the opera in 1780–81. He had been brought up in Salzburg, a small city-state that was, by the later eighteenth century, a cultural backwater. His father Leopold, as frustrated by the provincialism of Salzburg as his son was to be later, had determined that Wolfgang should receive a cosmopolitan musical and intellectual education, and he used his son's precocious talents as a boy to expose him to the cultures of Italy, France and England. Mozart's own sense of his cultural identity was accordingly, in many respects, confused. His astonishing powers of musical assimilation meant that he embraced the musical cosmopolitanism of the age with ease. But he also had a sense of his identity as a 'German' composer in a Germany that at this time only existed as a cultural rather than political entity, and moreover a cultural and linguistic entity that was deeply divided between the mainly Protestant north and the mainly Catholic south. In Paris in 1778 he had expressed his desire 'to do honour to the whole German nation', and on his way back to Salzburg from Paris had sought employment at the newly founded German National Theatre in Mannheim. But he soon realized that the possibilities for German opera in Mannheim were extremely limited, not least because the famous Mannheim orchestra had been transferred to Munich when the Elector of Mannheim became ruler of Bavaria in 1777. It was in Mannheim that Mozart became most frustrated with German culture and started to express his preference for writing French or Italian opera. *Idomeneo* is both at once, and it was Mozart's first really important break in the genre of opera, the form in which above all he sought to excel, and for which he had few opportunities in Salzburg.

Mozart seized the opportunity in *Idomeneo* to display his full, awesome powers. He was now, after all, writing for the virtuoso instrumental musicians of the erstwhile Mannheim orchestra, and the complexity of the score shows his relish for the possibilities this gave. And he turned to a French libretto for his new opera, having recently experienced French opera on his visit to Paris in 1778, when the war between the supporters of Gluck's operatic reforms and the supporters of the Italianate work of Piccinni was at its height. While Mozart admired Gluck greatly, and *Idomeneo* shows evidence of some Gluckian procedures, its musical forms are in other respects closer to the practices of Italian opera, with its predominance of self-contained arias, for which Mozart devised some of his most complex musical structures. The Act Three quartet, however, is neither French, nor Gluckian nor Italian, but uniquely Mozartian.

But *Idomeneo* draws on more than just a French libretto. It also reflects Mozart's engagement with the progressive social ideas of the French Enlightenment *philosophes* such as Voltaire, Diderot and Rousseau. On their first visit to Paris in 1763 the Mozart family had been taken up by the Franco-German *philosophe* Baron Friedrich Melchior Grimm, a close associate of both Diderot and Rousseau, and a key figure in the dissemination of French Enlightenment ideas to German-speaking lands. His interest in Mozart was almost certainly because the boy's astonishing musical precociousness was seen as evidence of a favourite Enlightenment theory that talents such as musicality were natural rather than learnt. On Mozart's return to Paris in 1778 his father Leopold had promised to give Wolfgang letters of introduction to both Diderot and d'Alembert, the editors of the *Encylopédie*, the crowning achievement of the French Enlightenment. And once in Paris, Wolfgang and his mother lodged with the writer Madame d'Épinay, who was Grimm's partner. Grimm himself had a close interest in opera and had been a key figure in the earlier controversy between Italian and French opera known as the *Querelle des Bouffons*, so Mozart would have been made very well aware of the passionate debates around the merits of the different operatic styles of his day.

The story of Idomeneus, the Cretan king who, returning home from Troy, promised to sacrifice the first human he met to propitiate the god Poseidon and ensure his safe return, subsequently meeting his own son, warrants only brief mentions in classical literature. But the subject matter of the story, the fateful vow to sacrifice a human being, takes many guises, and was widespread in eighteenth-century art. The best-known treatment of the theme in classical literature is found in the story of Agamemnon's sacrifice of his daughter Iphigenia to ensure the passage to Troy of the Greek fleet, becalmed on the island of Aulis, which had been the subject of a tragedy by Euripides and subsequently Racine. The stories of Iphigenia on Aulis and Iphigenia on Tauris, the latter of which also treats of human sacrifice, provided the basis for two of Gluck's most important French operas of 1774 and 1779, and for Goethe's play *Iphigenie auf Tauris,* begun in 1779. An obvious biblical counterpart to the Idomeneus story is the story of Abraham and Isaac. But the episode from the Book of Judges of the Jewish King Jephthah's vow to sacrifice the first human he meets if God grants him victory in battle, whereupon he meets his daughter, is also widespread in eighteenth-century art, best known from Handel's oratorio *Jephtha* of 1751, in which the unfortunate daughter, unnamed in the Bible,

11

is given the name Iphis, a clear reference to her classical counterpart Iphigenia.

To the Enlightenment *philosophes*, the object of whose contumely was above all the prevalence of religious superstition and credulity in modern society, the suggestion that the gods, or God, might demand human sacrifice was grist to the mill of their depiction of the cruelties of organised religion and its use of injunctions and sanctions based upon fear and cruelty. This was the reason for the prevalence of sacrifice stories in Enlightenment arts. In his campaign to 'écraser l'infâme' Voltaire found evidence of what he described as 'organised crime' in all religions, citing precisely the stories of Jephthah and Iphigenia in support of his argument against priestcraft: 'From Calchas, who murdered the daughter of Agamemnon [...] sacerdotal power has been disastrous to the world.' One of Voltaire's most high-profile interventions against religious infamy in his own day concerned the notorious Calas case of the 1760s, in which a Protestant father was wrongly convicted of murdering his son to prevent him converting to Catholicism. For Voltaire it was a clear case of judicial murder in the name of religion, and the case became the focal point for his campaigns, as well as being taken up by other supporters. Leopold Mozart's name is found on a subscription list for a print published by Grimm to raise money for the Calas family, indicating that the Mozart family must have been very familiar with such controversies.

For the Enlightenment, human sacrifice, in particular parental sacrifice, presented the starkest possible conflict between the laws of nature and the commands of religion. In Schiller's *Don Carlos*, published in 1787, the Grand Inquisitor demands that King Philip destroy his subversive son Don Carlos. When the king appeals to him that this would be a sin against nature, the old priest declares that the voice of nature has no worth before the commands of faith. Similarly in *Idomeneo* it is the High Priest who is obdurate in his insistence that Idomeneo must sacrifice his son.

A second common Enlightenment theme that occurs in *Idomeneo* is that of the danger of making, or believing oneself to be tied by, religious vows. A short story by Voltaire entitled *Le Taureau blanc*, published in two parts in 1773 and 1774, is yet another parental sacrifice story in which a king of Egypt vows to sacrifice his daughter if she mentions the name of her lover. When she does so, the king argues that vows must be upheld come what may. The tale warns against making, and believing oneself to be tied by, vows to God which contravene the laws of nature and society, an issue which was of the greatest significance to the *philosophes*. For the *philosophes*, who subscribed to a contractual view of social relations, vows were only valid when they were made freely between equals, and not under duress (as is Idomeneo's vow to Neptune). They often cited the scandal of women who were forced to take religious vows against their will and to become nuns – the subject of Diderot's novel *La Religieuse*, based upon a real-life case with which Friedrich Grimm and Madame d'Épinay had been involved in the 1760s. And as far as the *philosophes* were concerned, any vow made to God was not freely made. Diderot considered the distinction between religious vows and religious oaths to be so important that he included an entry in the *Encyclopédie* on the subject, stating that oaths are acceptable since they are engagements between two people 'who take God as a witness to what is being undertaken', as opposed to vows made to God himself, which, as Thomas Hobbes, a key proponent of contractual theory, had argued, was, 'impossible […] for we know not whether our Covenants be accepted or not'. In seventeenth-century England the playwright Aphra Behn, a supporter of absolutist monarchy, had argued that 'of all the sins incident to human nature, there is none of which Heaven has took so particular, visible or frequent notice, and revenge, as that of violated vows which never go unpunished'. But in Handel's *Jephtha*, written under a constitutional regime, the angel who stays the 'slaught'rous hand' of Jephtha declares that 'no vow can disannul the law of God'.

In Antoine Danchet's original libretto for *Idomenée* the gods are unrelenting, and Idamante has to die. Mozart and Varesco, his Italian collaborator in adapting the libretto, changed the ending. As the knife is raised, Ilia makes a dramatic entry to the scene and offers herself as victim to Neptune in place of Idamante. 'The gods are not tyrants; you are all false interpreters of the divine will,' she proclaims, a sentiment that almost exactly echoes the Iphigenie of Goethe's play *Iphigenie auf Tauris*, begun two years before *Idomeneo*, in which Iphigenie similarly argues that 'He who believes the gods to be bloodthirsty misunderstands them; he is only imputing to them his own fearsome desires'. Both Ilia and Iphigenie make leaps of faith at a crucial moment in their respective dramas that affirm the Enlightenment's belief that the moral laws of nature are upheld by a just God. Ilia's faith is indeed instantly upheld by Neptune's sudden incarnation and intervention to halt the sacrifice. Similarly, at the end of Gluck's *Iphigénie en Tauride*, the goddess Diana appears to confirm that her altars and laws have been sullied by human sacrifice. In all of these cases, there is a clear supposition that standing above any rules and laws made by kings and priests is a natural law which always overrides humanly decreed laws, to which appeal may be made. In *Idomeneo*, as in so much eighteenth-century thought and art, the ideal of nature, whether external or internal (as in the concept of human nature), is the guarantor of truth and justice. When natural laws are disturbed, nature reveals its distress through the violent storms and shipwrecks that are so prominent in the operas of Gluck and in *Idomeneo*. Those who stand on the side of justice recognize the beneficence of nature, as does Ilia in her aria 'Zeffiretti lusinghieri' ('Flattering zephyrs') at the beginning of Act Three, which takes place in a garden in which she sings to the gentle breezes. Those whose passions are 'unnatural' know both inner turmoil, as in the madness of Elettra, and also suffer nature's external physical turbulence directly: Elettra's wishful longing for gentle breezes to carry her and Idamante away from Crete is brutally interrupted by another storm which prevents the departure and tells us quite clearly that Elettra's jealous tribal desires for Idamante are not blessed by nature.

But *Idomeneo* is not only about the supplanting of superstitious religious beliefs. Like Aeschylus's *Oresteia*, it is about the super-session of outdated social structures based upon cycles of familial and tribal revenge and counter-revenge. The libretto upon which Mozart and Varesco based *Idomeneo* is a typical example of French classical drama, establishing a conflict between the passions and duty. Mozart's Ilia (a daughter of Troy, as her name indicates, taken captive by the victorious Greeks) is torn between her forbidden love for Idamante and the demands of vengeance for her family, who have been destroyed by the Greeks. Ilia refuses the imperative of vengeance, but Elettra, the sister of Iphigenia, whose fate is to become entangled in just such a spiral of revenge, reveals the cost of such vindictive emotions in her descent into madness. For Enlightenment modernizers, familial or tribal vengeance was an atavistic imperative that needed to be replaced by public justice or personal reconciliation, preferably based on an ideal of familial love. Indeed, two of Ilia's three arias are declarations of such love. In the first she laments the loss of her father and relatives and agonizes over the duty of vengeance. But in the second, 'Se il padre perdei' ('Though I have lost my father'), she transfers her filial devotion to Idomeneo, adopting him as a new father. As the victim she holds the key to the broader reconciliation between Greece and Troy that Elettra, who also loves Idamante, cannot accept.

Enlightenment political theorists placed such familial sentiment, a non-sexual bond of love, at the heart of the modern social order and embedded the family as a bulwark of a more gentle society in place of authoritarian systems of government based on arbitrary or punitive laws. The benign patriarch is one of the most widespread of Enlightenment subjects, evident in plays such as Diderot's *Le Père de famille*, or in a German version *Der deutsche Hausvater* of 1779 by Otto von Gemmingen, a writer well known to Mozart, and in the French painter Greuze's sentimental tableaus of paternal and familial love. Moreover, the modern subject was enjoined to see his or her ruler in a similarly benign paternal or maternal light. Writing in 1777, a visitor to Vienna noted the maternal sway of the Empress Maria Theresa, and the composer Carl Dittersdorf related in his autobiography how he had appealed to his employer the Bishop of Pressburg to call him his son, to which the Bishop apparently agreed with tears pouring down his cheeks.

Despite its supposed tenderness, this elevation of the patriarchal family as the vehicle of alternative authority within an increasingly individualistic society in fact creates enormous tensions and conflicts. Indeed, the father who sacrifices his son is in some ways merely enacting the reality of patriarchal authority in society. Some of these contradictions clearly coloured Mozart's own relationship with his father during the composition of *Idomeneo*. Leopold Mozart made inordinate demands on his son, loading him with responsibility for the well-being of his family and with an appalling sense of guilt for his longings for independence. At the end of Mozart's version of the drama, Idamante is made King of Crete in place of his father. But when Mozart wrote the opera he didn't know whether he would ever achieve the freedom from his own father's tyranny that this symbolizes. Many years after Mozart's death, his widow Constanze recalled that on a visit made by Wolfgang and herself to Leopold and Nannerl Mozart in Salzburg in 1783 the family had sung the great quartet from *Idomeneo*. Wolfgang had taken the role of Idamante, the son who must leave his homeland for exile abroad to escape being sacrificed by his father Idomeneo, sung by Leopold. But according to Constanze, Wolfgang 'was so overcome that he burst into tears and quit the chamber'. Surely he must have identified the operatic situation with his own revolt against the overbearing sacrificial demand of his father and with the fact that to obtain his freedom he had had to leave Salzburg and his family for exile and freedom in Vienna.

Idomeneo, re di Creta: the music

Julian Rushton

However you approach *Idomeneo* – as music, as theatre, as a document of its age – it remains one of Mozart's most extraordinary works. Yet it is not the product of his unaided genius. As a composer, part of a team, he responded to stimuli beyond his personal control: the terms of the Munich commission, the subject and libretto (not his choice, but supplied by the management), and the local performers (Kapellmeister Cannabich, the singers, dancers and members of the orchestra, of whom many were already well known to him). Luckily for Mozart, the Salzburg court chaplain Giambattista Varesco never came to Munich and dealt with the composer through Leopold Mozart. Luckily, too, for us: the Mozarts' letters are replete with information on the opera's progress, and Varesco's absence freed Mozart to intervene in the poet's domain, which included the libretto and the stage action.

Mozart moulded the opera for performance in consultation with his singers and also composed the obligatory ballet, which he could have left to a local hack, to preserve the unity of the evening's entertainment.[1] A three-act opera with ballet is a long evening; and in the end, Mozart had to make substantial cuts. Possibly the three Munich performances each contained different music. There is thus no definitive version of *Idomeneo*, something that only adds to its fascination. Conductors and directors have Mozart's implicit authority to omit certain arias, reduce the recitatives, and select variants made for the single Vienna performance, in 1786, tailored to a partly amateur cast and requiring a tenor instead of a castrato Idamante.

---

1. For a full account see Stanley Sadie, 'Genesis of an operone', in Julian Rushton (ed.), *W.A. Mozart: Idomeneo* (Cambridge: Cambridge University Press, 1993), 25–47.

17

The most interesting changes leading up to the Munich performances are those that show Mozart taking charge. At the climax
of Act Two, he pointed out that 'the storm isn't going to abate just
so that Herr Raaff [Anton Raaff, the tenor who created the role of
Idomeneo] can sing an aria [...] – it would be better to have a mere
recitative'.[2] Idamante's third-act aria, 'No la morte io non pavento'
('No, I do not fear death'), may have been cut and then restored
(perhaps the Elector wanted full value from his castrato), but it stops
the clock at the crux of the opera: the priest isn't going to defer the
sacrifice so the victim can sing an aria. While dropping the confidant
Arbace's arias in Acts Two and Three does no serious dramaturgical
damage, Mozart requested additional words for his recitative in Act
Three, because the original singer, Domenico de' Panzacchi, was a
capable actor. Third-act arias for Elettra and Idomeneo were also
dropped; they follow the oracle's merciful pronouncement, which
brings the action to a halt. Both singers had to be content with richly
expressive recitatives that fulfil a dramatic function by contrasting
the baffled fury of Elettra with the serenity of Idomeneo's abdication
speech. The following discussion is based on the original grand plan
of 1781, preserved in the libretto, noting variants as they occur.[3]

* * *

Act One

The superb overture prepares us for scenes of majesty, terror,
suffering and final reconciliation. The powerful opening arpeggio

2. See Julian Rushton, '"...hier wird es besser seyn – ein blosses Recitativ zu
machen": observations on recitative organization in Idomeneo', in Stanley
Sadie (ed.), Wolfgang Amadè Mozart (Oxford: Oxford University Press,
1996), 436–48.
3. Varesco insisted the libretto should be presented intact, whatever cuts were
made in the performance. The nineteenth-century Mozart edition (Breit-
kopf und Härtel, reprinted as a Kalmus miniature score) adheres as closely
as possible to the original plan. The new edition (Neue Mozart-Ausgabe)
tries to represent what was performed and includes the Vienna variants in
sequence, relegating cuts to the appendix. More recent studies following
rediscovery of the autograph score cast some doubt on the editor's decisions
(see Sadie, op. cit.).

[0a][4] is succeeded by a figure suggestive of turbulent seas [0b], to which a descending woodwind figure responds [0c]. A subsidiary theme [0d] stands out by its unusual tonality – A minor, quickly modulating to C major. It is unlikely that Mozart employed recurring motifs with Wagnerian deliberation, but motivic associations that may have arisen in the fever of composition have often been noticed and surely affect our interpretation. The rising arpeggio [0a] has been connected to several similar shapes, often in the main key, D major. The wind figure [0c] dominates the closing bars of the overture in a superbly controlled diminuendo. Closely related motifs recur so often that [0c] has been dubbed the 'Sacrifice' or 'Idamante' motif. Elements in the strangely isolated lyrical passage [0d] may be associated with Ilia and with passages in orchestral recitative where there are intimations of hope. This motivic network enhances the importance of the Trojan princess, whose self-sacrificing intrusion brings about the reconciliation of god and king and thus the happy ending (*lieto fine*) commanded, one must suppose, by the Munich court, to replace the horrific ending of the source libretto, Antoine Danchet's *Idomenée*.[5]

The overture's gentle ending prepares Ilia's first words, sung unaccompanied. Her feelings are explored in recitative enlivened by a multitude of appropriate musical responses from the orchestra, the first of this opera's unparalleled wealth of expressive orchestrally accompanied recitative. The aria, 'Padre, germani, addio!' ('Father, brothers, farewell!')[1a], is a binary form, the words being repeated, but more intensely. This is presumably the aria with which the prima donna Dorothea Wendling was, in Mozart's engaging tautology, 'arcicontentissima' ('very extremely content'), as well she might be, for this beautiful piece compactly expresses Ilia's anxious hesitation, her despairing cry of 'Grecia' ('Greece', cause of her exile), her qualms of conscience and the conflict of duty with love. When her thoughts turn to Idamante, the orchestra recalls the overture's characteristic figure [1b; cf. 0c].

4. Numbers in square brackets refer to the Thematic Guide on pp. 53–60 [Ed.].

5. Julian Rushton, 'A reconciliation motif in *Idomeneo*', in Dorothea Link (ed., with Judith Nagley), *Words about Mozart: Essays in Honour of Stanley Sadie* (Woodbridge: The Boydell Press, 2005), 21–32. On the change of emphasis in the libretto, see Don Neville, 'From *tragédie lyrique* to moral drama', in Rushton, *W.A. Mozart: Idomeneo*, 72–82. Danchet's libretto was set by André Campra (1660–1744) in 1712.

Ilia was the only character whose arias were not omitted in any revisions. Mozart had more difficulty with the young man who disturbs her peace of mind, for Idamante's music was restrained by the musical limitations he perceived in the singer, 'mio molto amato castrato [Vincenzo] dal Prato'. Idamante's first aria, 'Non ho colpa, e mi condanni' ('I am blameless, and you condemn me')[2], is nevertheless moving in its directness, establishing a vulnerable character, honest and of simple nobility. After a short introduction, it is mainly in a faster tempo, with murmuring clarinets and bassoons in the minor mode against an arching melody, as he says he will die from love. A version of 'his' motif [0c; cf. bar 32] introduces a closing section, and the aria is expanded by a fully recomposed repetition of the text and a conclusion of some brilliance. Idamante frees the Trojan prisoners; Cretan women and Trojan men provide interludes in the lively chorus, 'Godiam la pace' ('Let us enjoy peace')[3].

Arbace's announcement of Idomeneo's presumed death is supported by one of Mozart's most uncanny harmonic progressions, though its realization is left to the keyboard continuo. The orchestra characterizes Idamante's impetuous exit, Ilia's noble regret and Elettra's seething temper. Indeed, shortly afterwards the orchestra boils over, launching the powerfully orchestrated aria (with four horns), 'Tutte nel cor vi sento' ('I feel you all in my heart')[4], during which the 'Idamante' motif is tossed around by woodwind [0c; cf. bars 62, 123]: she would rather he were dead than married to anyone else. In an unprecedented masterstroke of musical dramaturgy, Mozart links the aria to the storm raging at sea. The full depth of the stage appears, revealing the sinking ship, drowning sailors and an apparition of Neptune. The key is C minor, unrelated to the preceding aria's D minor. But during the aria Mozart reflected Elettra's inchoate rage by interrupting its progress with a terrifying pause (one of many fierce diminished sevenths in this opera) and by recapitulating in the wrong key – C minor – before wrenching the music back to D minor in a rising sequence. The aria form runs its course, but the music never stops, plunging back to C minor and into the following chorus, 'Pietà Numi, pietà!' ('Mercy, O gods, mercy!')[5], with no change of tempo. Elettra is thus identified with hostile nature – or, in the context of Greek myth, with the hostile god.[6]

The libretto specifies that Idomeneo's fatal vow is now shown in pantomime, and Mozart calms the orchestra in a rapid but controlled diminuendo prior to the king making land and dismissing his followers. The following recitatives were subject to severe pruning, mainly because neither the elderly Anton Raaff (Idomeneo) nor dal Prato (Idamante) could act with sufficient animation and intensity to justify Varesco's verbosity. But Raaff at sixty-six could still deliver a fine aria. Like Idamante's, it is in two tempi, slow then fast, with extended passages in the minor mode; the orchestration is a little fuller. Both arias rail at the harshness of fate. Idomeneo's depression is expressed by his drooping first phrase [6a], 'Vedrommi intorno' (I will see around me), with its emphasis on the subdominant (marked by the B flat). Woodwind echoes evoke the ghost by which he fears he will be haunted, and the Allegro [6b] registers impassioned self-pity.

As with Elettra's aria, the music drives through the vocal cadence into the recitative, leaving no time for applause. Idomeneo sees the victim approaching; gradually (depending on how much recitative is included) he and his son realize who the other is, and the orchestra explodes into action, with arpeggios of astonishment (reminiscent of [0a]), phrases of tenderness, stern admonition as Idomeneo banishes his son and wailing woodwind for the son's despair. Idamante's aria, 'Il padre adorato' ('My beloved father')[7], is all fast, and some of its orchestral character suggests insecurity, like the preceding orchestral recitative. A rapid modulation from D minor to C minor (from bar 20) recalls the mental disturbance of Elettra.

Convention required an intermezzo before Act Two, an opportunity to fill the stage with chorus and dancers, deployed here with dramatic irony: Idomeneo is joyously welcomed home, but while his heart is breaking the music depicts only the people's joy. Each act of *Idomeneo* contains a march. The first [8] is the loudest

---

6. Craig Ayrey finds motivic connections between the storm at sea and Elettra's third-act aria, which is also in C minor, concluding that 'Mozart's treatment of Elettra forms a psychological and ideological sub-plot in which *opera seria* is nascent music drama'. 'Elettra's first aria and the storm scene', in Rushton, *W.A. Mozart: Idomeneo*, 137–52.

and most confident, in the key of the overture. There follows a
choral 'Ciaccona' [9], with solo episodes and presumably dancing;
more dances may have been inserted at this point.

Act Two

The beginning of Act Two was radically revised for the Vienna
performance in 1786. In 1781 a simple dialogue leads to Arbace's first
aria, 'Se il tuo duol' ('If your grief')[10a]. Suited to a well-intentioned
confidant who was also a highly trained virtuoso – although by
now, at forty-seven, Panzacchi was a little over the hill – it would
fit without incongruity in a much earlier opera, such as *Lucio Silla*
(1772). Yet at this point we hardly need the 1786 alternative, a second
confrontation between Ilia and Idamante, although his sentiments
of love account for Ilia's happiness in the next scene. It is a poor
distribution of solos that gives us Idamante's third complaint before
anyone else has a second aria. The violin obbligato composed for
Mozart's friend Count Hatzfeld somewhat overshadows the tenor
voice, and the two-tempo rondò form [10b] belongs to a later style:
Mozart set the same words more eloquently a few months later for
the farewell concert of his first Susanna, Nancy Storace.[7]

The action resumes when Ilia addresses her second aria to Idomeneo.
Sure of Idamante's love, even though she does not acknowledge
it, she declares with the utmost tenderness that she has found a
second home, a second father, 'Se il padre perdei' ('Though I have
lost my father')[11a, b]. Mozart treated his wind-playing friends to
an obbligato quartet (flute, oboe, horn and bassoon), providing an
instrumental halo for the singer's beautifully spun line. The contrast
with the light instrumentation of Arbace's aria and the trumpets and
timpani in Idomeneo's aria in the next scene is carefully calculated.

The core of Act Two is Idomeneo's soliloquy. His thoughts are
so perturbed by Ilia's declaration that phrases from her aria are
transformed within his recitative [12a; cf. 11b], surely one of the
most imaginative dramatic uses of the orchestra before the nineteenth
century. The aria 'Fuor del mar' ('Though saved from the sea')
[12b] is of show-stopping virtuosity, its arpeggio theme inverting

---

7. 'Ch'io mi scordi di te – Non temer amato bene' (K505), this time with piano
   obbligato played by Mozart.

the very start of the opera [0a] and its dotted rhythms recalling the majesty of a French Baroque overture. Yet as in his first aria [6] the opening subsides, as if discouraged, through the subdominant (to G, by way of C natural). Energy returns, with a fine display of passagework. A simpler version was prepared for the 1786 singer and not (as sometimes stated) because Raaff was short of breath or less agile than in former times. Idomeneo's thoughts move from self-pity to resolution: he will defy the cruel gods; let them wreck him, not his innocent child (a heart-stopping modulation at the centre of the aria: 'Or gli vieta il naufragar' , from A minor to F sharp minor). He strives in vain to save his son, but the aria makes plain his noble intention to sacrifice himself (if possible) and the strength of character that makes this resolution plausible.

As with the intermezzo after Act One, dramatic irony colours our response to a scene of contentment. Mozart customarily orchestrated at least one aria per opera for strings alone, usually for a minor character. Elettra is hardly that, and Mozart's choice here is surely intended to mark a contrast to the powerful wind writing of her first aria, with its slightly deranged flute arpeggios. Elettra's love for Idamante is no less heartfelt for being governed by egotism, and the original singer, Elisabeth Wendling, possessed the versatility required to switch from furious energy to elegant cantabile and fluid passagework: the paired notes curve seductively as she imagines herself wooing Idamante away from Ilia, 'Idol mio' ('My idol')[13]. The cadence leads directly into a short march, which takes four bars to find its home key [14]. The brass mutes had to be brought from Salzburg by Leopold Mozart. Elettra continues singing happily through the first section; as the procession enters, the brass mutes are removed for the last reprise.

If anything could be more serene than Elettra's aria, it is the following chorus, to which she contributes a central solo, 'Placido è il mar' ('The sea is calm') [15]. As later in Così fan tutte, Mozart evokes a calm sea and sweet breezes in the key of E major, the orchestra softened by using flutes and clarinets but no oboes and bassoons. Tragedy seems far away until the king and Idamante enter, the son desperate to know how he has displeased his father. He is told to leave the island and responds with a heartfelt plea for some sign of affection, introducing an extended and moving trio [16], for which

Mozart rearranged the voice parts in 1786 to accommodate a tenor Idamante.[8] When the voices join, it is to ask the gods' favour, which is immediately and violently refused: Mozart interrupts the expected musical closure by a passage that daringly matches the stage effects specified in the libretto, which include a tempest, lightning and a swelling ocean. What follows must have tested his orchestra and chorus to the limit, as the terrified people, confronted with a monster emerging from the sea, demand to know who has offended the gods: the uproar halts three times for massive diminished seventh chords from the winds. Since Mozart rejected the librettist's first idea, that Raaff should respond with a mere aria, the last wind blast and choral outcry [17] are answered by an impressive recitative, during which the tempest does gradually abate. Idomeneo's ringing declaration that he alone is culpable brings back the trumpets, drums and D major of 'Fuor del mar', after which his moving evocation of the unfortunate victim is supported by orchestral eloquence rather than nature-painting. If they kill the innocent, the gods cannot claim to be just. This blasphemy terrifies the people who scatter in a chorus which the librettist said would have to serve as the intermezzo. Indeed, there is no place, even with dramatic irony, for any cheerful chorus and dance. Instead Mozart produced a distorted reprise of the overture, with a rising *minor* arpeggio [18], and a response in the orchestra that is both a threat from the sea and a memory of the 'Idamante' motif. Yet, as the act comes to an end, the last sound heard is D major, and a hint of hope; the final bars precisely anticipate the opening of Act Three and the scene for Ilia, who unknowingly holds the fate of Crete in her hands.

Act Three

Ilia's short recitative repeats the close of the previous chorus, and this idea generates the opening of her aria, in E major, 'Zeffiretti lusinghieri' ('Flattering zephyrs')[19], still the key for soft breezes and a calm sea, again without oboes, but with flutes and clarinets. The interplay of wind instruments with the voice is different from

---

8. Singing the castrato version an octave lower sounds intermittently terrible. Tenor versions of the trio and quartet are missing from the old edition, but are included in the Neue Mozart-Ausgabe.

the Act Two obbligato [11b], but resembles the sensitive interjection of wind phrases into Idamante's second aria. Ilia does recall her Act Two aria almost to the point of quotation, by a series of wide intervals, emblematic of longing [cf. No. 11, the reprise from bar 76; No. 19, the parallel passage from bar 77]. Again the cadence is broken into by the entry of Idamante. Ilia's surprise leads her to drop her guard and admit her love; simple recitative mutates, as so often in this opera, into expressive recitative accompanied by strings. This in turn merges seamlessly into a duet [20a], yet another piece that does not begin on its principal, or tonic, harmony. In 1786 it was replaced by a shorter movement for soprano and tenor, in the same key and opening with the same idea, but – perhaps significantly – this time with Ilia taking the lead [20b].

The lovers are surprised by Idomeneo and Elettra. Confident now in Ilia's love, Idamante, demanding to know why his father rejects him, adopts a tone of voice and a tonality as far removed as possible from the duet; that was in A, but his speech and the subsequent quartet are in E flat. During a particularly tense recitative the harmony moves back to A, then prepares for the quartet in E flat [21]. Idamante, crushed by his father's continuing coldness, stares into a loveless future in exile. The quartet begins with him alone, a finely arched phrase which, although in the major mode, comes over as the epitome of dejection. This even Ilia cannot alleviate, despite raising the tonality to its dominant, and replacing the leaden steps of the string accompaniment to Idamante's speech with livelier figures (closing bars of [21]). Idomeneo and Elettra sing aside, he blaming the gods, she wanting vengeance; the lovers' voices join, then all four sing together in equal suffering, but – at least from Elettra – without mutual sympathy. The second part covers the same musical and textual ground with increased intensity, and in a final masterstroke Mozart has the four voices pause on a dominant chord, leaving their cadence incomplete. Idamante repeats half his first speech, ending inconclusively; the orchestra is left to cadence gently, alone and this time without interruption.

Mozart was right to be proud of this movement, his masterly contribution to a relatively new fashion for substantial ensembles in *opera seria*.[9] He insisted to Raaff that while the individual singer's

---

9. See Marita P. McClymonds, 'The Great Quartet in *Idomeneo* and the Italian *opera seria* tradition', in Sadie, *Wolfgang Amadè Mozart*, 449–76.

capabilities should be involved in creating an aria, ensembles are the composer's domain, and vocal effects would be misplaced. The quartet's exploration of despair and human powerlessness is developed by sheer musical beauty, and such a combination might well reduce anyone to tears, as evidently it once did Mozart, perhaps because it revived memories of the unadulterated happiness he seems to have experienced in writing this opera.

What could possibly follow? The temperature must be lowered; and this could all too easily be achieved by an aria for the confidant. But the following scene cannot simply be omitted; the recitative is one of the most remarkable in a score packed with such passages. Arbace's lament at the state of Crete is introduced by a phrase of striking eloquence [22a]. What it speaks of may even be hope [cf. 19], which Arbace himself expresses, 'Io spero ancora' ('I still hope'), amid phrases that penetrate our feelings by an acute dissonance that results from close imitation between the string parts: it isn't often in eighteenth-century music that we hear B flat, B natural and C simultaneously [22b]. This splendid recitative can well stand alone; and it is only now, with an aria orchestrated only for strings, 'Se colà ne' fati è scritto' ('If thus it is written in the fates') [22c], that the temperature is actually lowered. Perhaps the original audience, not used to (for instance) Verdi, Wagner or Berg, could have found in this aria a welcome relief from dramatic music of well-nigh unbearable intensity.

The libretto now indicates a grand public gathering. The music is barely coherent: a heroic C major reminiscence of the overture [23a; cf. 0a], an abrupt descent, an unmeasured silence; then in a remote key (A flat) a reminiscence of the music of hope or reconciliation; then feverish textures and rapid decay, before the abrupt descent assumes the fixed motivic shape that punctuates the tremendous speech of the High Priest [23b]. Idomeneo's resistance is broken; he reveals the victim's name to a sensitively harmonized version of the 'Idamante' motif [23c]. Stark woodwind chords and a lone note from an oboe underline the pathos of this terrible moment. The people, and even the priest, are awestruck; the slow chorus, 'Oh voto tremendo!' ('Oh terrible vow!')[24a], expands C minor, a tragic key in the context of this opera. Yet even here, at the very end, C major brings a pale ray of hope, a distant reminder of music associated with Ilia [24b; cf. 0d, 19].

Mozart's resourcefulness, and his sense of what matches a dramatic context, can be exemplified by the three marches in *Idomeneo*. The first [8] is cheerful, heroic and loud; the second [12] is a processional crescendo; the third [25] is lightly scored, typical of the religious marches of Gluck's operas and Mozart's own later *Zauberflöte*. Ritual mode is maintained in the remarkable prayer (*Cavatina con coro*) for Idomeneo and the priests – a solemn wind chant and an eloquent plea from the king, 'Accogli, oh re del mar, i nostri voti' ('Receive our vows, O king of the sea') [26], to which a chorus of priests responds in a drear ritualistic monotone.

A trumpet fanfare, in a D major sounding the more brilliant for coming after the *Cavatina*'s F, shatters the ritual atmosphere. Arbace proclaims that the hero Idamante has killed the monster; and he enters, the dutiful son dressed for sacrifice [27a], accepting the gods' will with allusions to 'his' motif [27b]. Idomeneo responds with the orchestra apparently quoting the eloquent opening of Arbace's recitative [27c; cf. 22a]. The dialogue of father and son, as in Act One, was subjected to cuts, the limited acting ability of the original singers being liable to try the patience of the audience. The bustling accompaniment to Idamante's aria [27d] does nothing to disguise the cessation of the action. This piece is somewhat more old-fashioned in style than his Act One arias; the fast D major, lightly orchestrated, and the elegant slow middle section might both, like Arbace's arias, have come from an earlier period. Again, Mozart elides the cadence with the following dialogue in recitative. At the critical moment Ilia appears, her recitative restoring harmonic and dramatic intensity; one chord progression, sequentially repeated, corresponds to Arbace bringing bad news [3b], but this time the chords are projected by string tremolo, while stabbing accents mark each change of harmony. The self-sacrificing argument between the lovers was prolonged by another stirring passage which Mozart felt obliged to cut before the 1781 performances.

As Idamante suggests they should die together, and Ilia protests that she alone should die, 'Heaven' intervenes; the oracle pronounces forgiveness. Mozart wanted trombones to create the effect of an otherworldly intervention, taking advantage of their association with the church. The extra cost was probably refused, despite Mozart (on his own admission) speaking rudely to the theatre intendant, Count Seeau. Mozart was forced to compose a version of the oracle's speech without them, substituting clarinets, bassoons and horns. It appears that he had already set versions of the oracle three times, abbreviating the text to a bare minimum. Only the fuller versions, beginning 'Ha vinto Amore' ('Love has conquered') [28], make it clear that the god's insistence that Idomeneo fulfil his vow by sacrificing Idamante has been conquered by the power of love. Mozart perhaps felt his audience, well versed in neo-classical drama, could work this out; after this tremendous initial impact (especially with trombones), a long oracular pronouncement would pay diminishing returns ('if the Ghost's speech in *Hamlet* weren't so long, it would be even more effective'[10]). As normally performed, the speech begins with swelling chords for trombones (as in [28]), but one version has a sturdy dotted rhythm instead.

Whichever version is used, the human response is haloed by a high woodwind chord. The relief and delight of the king, his son, Ilia and Arbace are swept aside by Elettra. Her recitative, which exists in two versions, one intended for use when the aria is omitted, includes wind instruments to add strength and colour to the orchestral gestures that underscore her impotent railing at fate. Her first aria began on the dominant; by starting her last on a subdominant (F minor) Mozart ratchets up the tension still more in the opening bars, 'D'Oreste, d'Aiace' ('Of Orestes, of Ajax')[29]. It is not all fury; she mourns, echoed by woodwind, before returning to her opening mood with giddy syncopation and a frenetic shower of staccato scales from top C.[11]

As if numbed, the orchestra settles on a chord of E flat, then embarks on a gentle but motivically rich passage of imitation [30a]. Idomeneo's abdication, addressed to his people (those the monster has spared), is given a rare eloquence through the orchestral interventions, including clarinets as the only woodwind, with a pair of horns (where Elettra had four horns, flutes, oboes, bassoons *and* trumpets and timpani). Mozart's sense of colour, as well as various orchestral motifs, connects this music to gentle Ilia whom, with Idamante, the retiring king commends to his subjects. The happy

---

10. Letter from Mozart to his father, 29th November 1781. They had recently seen *Hamlet* in Salzburg.

11. Elettra leaves in a rage ('parte infuriata'), but nothing in the libretto suggests that she commits suicide, as is sometimes stated.

ending seems arbitrary on paper, but in sound it convinces by summing up, without actually repeating, the music associated with Idamante, Ilia, hope and reconciliation. E flat, relative of C minor, banishes the turbulent and irrational. It is strangely moving as, indeed, is Idomeneo's three-part aria, 'Torna la pace al core' ('Peace returns to my heart')[30b], if the performers and audience are equal to such an expansion of the mood of peace and harmony; this too Mozart had to cut before the 1781 performances after he and Raaff had plagued the librettist for a better text.

With or without the aria, the king falls serenely silent in the key of B flat. Mozart returns without transition to the main key, the brilliant D major of military and courtly celebration, for a chorus [31] with a danced interlude, and a particularly fine chaconne [32]; both refer thematically to the opening of Idomeneo's central aria 'Fuor del mar' [12b]. There are other dances, to which the Köchel catalogue gave a different number (367) from the main opera (366). It is hard to be certain how many of these were actually used, and most modern performances conclude with the chorus in praise of love and marriage: 'Scenda Amor, scenda Imeneo'.

* * *

Idomeneo is the apogee of the eighteenth-century 'reform' opera, evolved by several composers including Jommelli, Traetta, Holzbauer and especially Gluck, who continued the reform by revolutionizing French tragic opera. Beside Gluck's austere programme, in which the composer was reduced to being the mere colourist of the poet's design, Mozart – not long before a teenage composer of successful *opera seria* on traditional lines – may appear to be backsliding. He later pronounced that poetry should be music's obedient servant; but he always allowed the strengths (and weaknesses) of singers to determine many aspects of his arias which to a Gluckist or post-Wagnerian sensibility may seem unnecessarily extended. But in important respects, notably the dynamism of the opera's continuity between aria and recitative, the recurrence of musical ideas that hint at leitmotif and the wealth of expressive orchestral recitative, Mozart exceeded Gluck and his immediate successors (Salieri, Piccinni, Johann Christian Bach) by a considerable distance.

The earliest English critical tribute to *Idomeneo* to treat it on its own terms was by Edward J. Dent. In *Mozart's Operas* (1913), he devoted more space to *Idomeneo* than to *Le nozze di Figaro*, and emphasized the 'nobility and dignity of the entire conception'. Many years later, Dent supervised performances of *Idomeneo* in Cambridge, and he came to regard it as an ideal work, one that set a standard of seriousness in musical and stage presentation, an opera essential for the education of new generations of singers, conductors and directors. To that one can only say 'Amen'.

A Brief Performance History

Gary Kahn

Mozart wrote two versions of *Idomeneo*. The first was commissioned for the court in Munich and featured a castrato, Vincenzo dal Prato, as Idamante, in addition to two soprano and three tenor roles. It was performed at the Cuvilliés-Theater on 29th January 1781, two days after Mozart's twenty-fifth birthday, and then twice more the following month. The second version was made for a single private performance with aristocratic amateur singers at Prince Auersperg's palace in Vienna on 13th March 1786. This version was shorter, incorporating some new material but with more omitted; the role of Idamante was rewritten for a tenor. Mozart seems to have retained a special affection for the work, but it was not revived again in his lifetime.

Following the initial performances in Munich and Vienna, productions of the opera in a version that Mozart would have recognized as his own were few until the middle of the twentieth century. The work was perceived, not entirely accurately, as an example of *opera seria*, which came to be regarded as an outmoded eighteenth-century form. Hence, performances throughout most of the nineteenth and early twentieth centuries were infrequent; all were substantially altered, cut and 'improved upon' to meet what was perceived as contemporary taste. The most extensive and best-known of these revisions was one made by Richard Strauss for a production at the Wiener Staatsoper in 1931 to mark the 150th anniversary of the work's premiere. Strauss adored the work, but nonetheless used a new libretto in German by Lothar Wallerstein, which changed Elettra's name to Ismene (a priestess rather than Agamemnon's daughter), rewrote the score and introduced original material in recognizably Straussian style.

31

It was not until after the Second World War that *Idomeneo* began to be performed at all often outside the German-speaking world or in anything close to its original eighteenth-century form. It is perhaps ironic that a large part of this change should have stemmed from a production in the United Kingdom, a country where it remained so relatively unappreciated that Covent Garden did not give its first performance of the work until 1978. There had been non-professional British staged performances in Glasgow in 1934, Falmouth in 1937 (which came to London for one performance in 1938) and by the Cambridge University Music Society in 1939 and Oxford University Opera Club in 1949, but it was not until 1951 at the Glyndebourne Festival that the work received its first British professional production. This was in an edition prepared by the Austrian composer and musicologist Hans Gál, which observed Mozart's intentions more closely than had been done since the composer's death.

Glyndebourne adopted changes Mozart made for the 1786 Vienna performance, with a tenor Idamante, a less difficult version of Idomeneo's Act Two aria, 'Fuor del mar', and many cuts, including both of Arbace's arias. The production was an immediate critical and popular success. Glyndebourne already had an established reputation as a Mozart house and, indeed, had championed at its first Festival in 1934 the then almost universally neglected *Così fan tutte*. This dedication to Mozart, together with the generous and thorough rehearsal schedule that the Festival afforded, ensured a committed team of artists working together in a way that began the rehabilitation of the work. The production was led by the established Glyndebourne Mozart team of conductor Fritz Busch and director Carl Ebert, with neo-classical scenery and elegant costumes by Oliver Messel that were both extremely decorative and theatrically effective. The cast in 1951 included Richard Lewis as Idomeneo, Sena Jurinac as Ilia, Birgit Nilsson as Elettra and Léopold Simoneau as Idamante. The production was revived at Glyndebourne in 1952, 1956, 1959 and 1964, and at the Edinburgh Festival in 1953. After Busch's death following the 1951 Festival, performances were conducted by John Pritchard (with some in 1959 also by Peter Gellhorn), and revival casts included Elisabeth Grümmer as Ilia in 1956 and the young Luciano Pavarotti as Idamante and Gundula Janowitz as Ilia in 1964.

The 1951 Salzburg Festival also presented a new production, conducted by Georg Solti and directed by Josef Gielen. In contrast to Glyndebourne's restitution of much of Mozart's score the same year, this was a version so truncated that the opera was reduced to a single act. It was not a notable success. The Mozart bicentenary in 1956, however, prompted houses, principally in Germany, to mount a number of new productions, most notably in Munich, Hanover, Essen and Augsburg, as well as a more complete one than in 1951 at that year's Salzburg Festival, directed by Oscar Fritz Schuh. Carl Ebert also directed a reworking of his 1951 Glyndebourne production in 1956 for the Berlin Städtische Oper. As the opera became better known, eminent conductors such as Karl Böhm and Robert Heger began to champion its cause. The editions that were used generally featured a tenor Idamante, and productions at this time remained largely neo-classical in style.

This remained the case as the opera began to gain currency and the number of productions increased. Established and emerging international singers such as Ludwig Suthaus as Idomeneo in Berlin (1957) and Elisabeth Söderström as Ilia in Stockholm (also 1957) began to appear in the opera and the early 1960s saw performances by Elisabeth Grümmer and Pilar Lorengar as Ilia (and Grümmer later in the decade as Elettra) and Waldemar Kmentt as Idomeneo (later as Arbace and, later still, as the High Priest). In the United Kingdom, Colin Davis began his long association with the complete opera by conducting the first professional production in London for the Sadler's Wells Opera Company in 1962. This was in a fuller edition of the work than most being used on the continent at the time, albeit still with a tenor Idamante, some cuts and sung in English. Another champion of the work, Benjamin Britten, made his own edition of the score for a production with his English Opera Group for the Aldeburgh Festival in 1969. This was also sung in English, with Peter Pears in the title role, and had, unusually for the time, a soprano Idamante, sung here by Anne Pashley. Performances took place at Blythburgh Church following the burning-down of the Maltings concert hall on the opening night of the festival that year. The production was directed by Colin Graham and subsequently filmed by the BBC at the London Opera Centre.

The neo-classical look of stage settings for *Idomeneo* such as those seen at Glyndebourne in 1951 and in many subsequent productions was beginning to give way by the mid-1960s to more timeless and even semi-abstract set designs. There was, certainly within mainland Europe, a general movement away from primarily decorative stage designs in opera, and singers' gestures and acting styles were also becoming less mannered. More emphasis was being placed on a psychological exploration of the characters in opera, as well as the wider political and social dimensions to be found in the works themselves. Productions made increasing dramatic demands of singers, and the role of the director in opera became progressively more important as directors and designers began investigating the contemporary relevance of the operas on which they worked.

Another development which affected the perception and performance of *Idomeneo* was the publication of the critical edition of the score in 1972 as part of the Neue Mozart-Ausgabe, under the editorship of Daniel Heartz, himself a particular advocate for the opera and the author of many important critical studies of aspects of the work. A fresh awareness of the work's genesis began to inform performances. In particular, an appreciation of the structural shape of Mozart's original Munich version, the musical advantages of having a soprano Idamante (particularly in the ensembles) and a more general understanding of the pragmatic reasons for Mozart's changes to his original 1781 score, led to more performances using a fuller version of the opera. These were much nearer to that heard at its Munich performances and, in many cases, restored music that Mozart, perhaps reluctantly, had to cut. When Charles Mackerras conducted the Glen Byam Shaw production (formerly under Colin Davis) from Sadler's Wells in 1970, following the company's move to the London Coliseum two years previously, it featured not only a female Idamante, Josephine Barstow, but also appoggiaturas and ornamentation that were evidence of an awareness of period performing practice and a harbinger of far-reaching changes that were to come in the performance of the opera over the following forty years.

Another significant event came in 1974 in Cologne with the first appearance of a production directed and designed by Jean-Pierre Ponnelle that would be seen in various versions and many revivals in major opera houses throughout the world over the course of the next twenty years. It introduced *Idomeneo* to new audiences, not least those in the United States, where the work had previously hardly been heard. This production was based on the original Munich version, albeit with substantial cuts and shorn of the concluding ballet. At the first performances in Cologne, the mezzo-soprano Idamante was Delia Wallis, and the rest of the cast included Werner Hollweg as Idomeneo and Lucia Popp as Ilia. Ponnelle's basic design feature was a huge rock-like mask of Neptune at the rear of the stage, which dominated the opera and set the interaction of the principal characters, as well as the chorus, into sharp relief. Ponnelle's direction of the characters, all dressed in variations of eighteenth-century baroque costume, was intensely human. The opera emerged strongly with a message of hope that a more enlightened world would follow Idomeneo's abdication in favour of Idamante and Ilia. Elettra was clearly seen as a representative of another, older and more vengeful order that could not survive. In Ponnelle's experienced and sympathetic hands, the stiff conventions of *opera seria* that had characterized earlier productions gave way to vivid and truthful emotions movingly conveyed. The production was soon afterwards also seen in San Francisco and Chicago. Productions at the Met and Salzburg followed shortly, as well as one by Zurich Opera, who also made visits with it to Vienna and Athens.

In the UK, *Idomeneo* was finally presented at Covent Garden in 1978. The production was directed by Götz Friedrich in monumental block-like designs by Stefanos Lazaridis that reconfigured them-selves ominously in the course of the action. With Colin Davis conducting, the cast included Stuart Burrows as Idomeneo, Yvonne Kenny as Ilia, Magdalena Cononovici as Elettra and, perhaps most importantly, Janet Baker as Idamante. The performances met with great acclaim and, with only one cast change – that of Elizabeth Vaughan as Elettra – the production was revived the following season.

Two years later, in 1980, Nikolaus Harnoncourt conducted the Ponnelle production in Zurich, and then in Vienna and Athens. The prevailing orchestral tradition of playing smoothly and with a lot of vibrato that had built up long after Mozart's own time was radically rethought. Harnoncourt's already considerable experience of working with period instruments was brought to bear on these performances. His orchestra used modern instruments, but played with gut strings, wooden drumsticks and narrow-bore trombones, and the music took on a fresh immediacy, excitement and even roughness. Over the next thirty years, it became increasingly difficult for conductors not to take account of such fundamental rethinking of how music of this period should be played.

At the same time as the period performance movement was making its presence felt, another development was taking place in opera houses around the world which, beginning in Germany, would bring about a profound change in the presentation of operas from all eras. A deconstructive post-modern school introduced new and radical approaches to opera production. Operas were frequently taken out of historically distant periods and staged in contemporary or near-contemporary clothes and settings. These productions took opera-goers out of the comfort zone of what Brecht had described as 'culinary theatre', and often deprived audiences of the pleasure of watching attractive productions in picturesque designs and period costumes. One of the first of these approaches to *Idomeneo* was directed by the East German Ruth Berghaus, herself a former director at Brecht's Berliner Ensemble, at the Berlin Staatsoper in 1981. It had semi-abstract designs by Peter Sykora and featured a trident-wielding Neptune striding across the stage at various points, showing no regard for the sufferings of the characters in the opera. Berghaus's fellow East German Harry Kupfer followed with a production in Stuttgart in 1984, which was similarly bleak in its setting for the portrayal of the drama.

Such interventionist productions were becoming increasingly common in Europe, as were more performances informed by the period practice movement, although not in the USA, where audiences and managements have traditionally been more conservative. A lavish version of the Ponnelle production, conducted by James Levine and with Luciano Pavarotti as Idomeneo, Ileana Cotrubas as Ilia, Frederica von Stade as Idamante and Hildegard Behrens as Elettra, arrived at the Metropolitan Opera, New York, in 1982 and was subsequently released on video. There have been many Met revivals since, in several of which Plácido Domingo has appeared as Idomeneo. In 1996 Domingo also recorded the role on CD with Levine conducting the Met Orchestra and Cecilia Bartoli as Idamante.

Glyndebourne introduced a new production in 1983 with Trevor Nunn's first venture into opera in John Napier's Japanese-influenced designs. This production, which was also televised and later released on video, was conducted by Bernard Haitink, featuring Philip Langridge as Idomeneo and Carol Vaness as Elettra, and continued the Glyndebourne tradition of casting a tenor Idamante, in spite of the growing practice elsewhere of using a soprano or mezzo-soprano in the role. The production met with considerable acclaim. It would be a few more years before period performing practice or a radical production of the opera arrived in Sussex.

In Europe, by contrast, productions were becoming more extreme. A deconstructed staging by Peter Mussbach in Kassel in 1984 infuriated many at its premiere by introducing extraneous childlike design elements and a mezzo-soprano to sing the High Priest. With the increasing adoption of more material from the original 1781 version, the concluding Act Three ballet, so long neglected, was also now finding its way back into performances, even if not always in full. In Vienna in 1987, Johannes Schaaf directed a production designed by David Fielding and conducted by Nikolaus Harnoncourt which included the final ballet, during which Idamante and Ilia attempted (and failed) to escape from the responsibilities of leadership imposed on them at the end of the opera. The ballet was also included in an important concert performance at the Queen Elizabeth Hall in London that same year, when Simon Rattle, already a world-class conductor but not one previously associated with period performing practice in opera, appeared with the original-instrument Orchestra of the Age of Enlightenment. The performance, featuring Philip Langridge as Idomeneo, Arleen Augér as Ilia, Diana Montague as Idamante and Carol Vaness as Elettra, had considerable influence. A challenging new production conducted by Jeffrey Tate and directed by Johannes Schaaf with sets by Hans Schavernoch then appeared at Covent Garden in 1989, portraying a harsh autocratic world indifferent to human suffering. Part of Act Three was played out in a lime-green burnt-out wasteland, Arbace killed himself after his second aria and, as in Schaaf's production in Vienna two years before, it was by no means clear at the end of the opera, which in this production also included about half of the ballet music, that a happy future lay ahead for Idamante and Ilia. As if in reaction, the English Bach Festival presented a single performance of the work on a Sunday at Covent Garden later that season in as faithful a reproduction as could be afforded of the 1781 first production, with a succession of backdrops reproducing Lorenzo Quaglio's original designs and reconstructed authentic dance movements to accompany the ballet.

In 1990 John Eliot Gardiner, the English Baroque Soloists and the Monteverdi Choir performed a concert version at the Queen Elizabeth Hall with Anthony Rolfe Johnson as Idomeneo, Sylvia McNair as Ilia, Anne Sofie von Otter as Idamante, Hillevi Martinpelto as Elettra, Nigel Robson as Arbace and Glenn Winslade as the High Priest. This was subsequently released on CD and was the first recording to feature period instruments. It was also the most complete recording so far of the 1781 score (some of it in appendices to permit listeners at home to construct their own version). As with 1981's Harnoncourt recording with the orchestra of the Zurich Opera House, informed as that was by Harnoncourt's own experience of working with period instruments, the release of these discs was to prove extremely influential. Their commercial success led to a more knowledgeable audience worldwide being able to appreciate the opera in a form closer to Mozart's original intentions than had previously been possible.

By the early 1990s, productions of *Idomeneo* were appearing with increasing regularity. One, directed by Frank Corsaro for Los Angeles Opera in 1990, engaged directly with the putative autobiographical element in the opera by dressing Idamante as Wolfgang and Idomeneo as Leopold Mozart. In 1991 (the bicentenary of Mozart's death), there were revivals of productions by Ponnelle at the Met (now in the hands of his chief assistant Lesley Koenig following Ponnelle's death), by Schaaf in Vienna, by Trevor Nunn at Glyndebourne and by Nikolaus Lehnhoff in Salzburg. The same year also saw new productions directed by Harry Kupfer at the Komische Oper in Berlin, by Howard Davies for Welsh National Opera and by Peter Mussbach for the Holland Festival. Both Cambridge University Opera Society and the Oxford

University Opera Club put on performances that year, the former in concert form and the latter in what was claimed to be the first staged performance in modern times with period instruments. A host of new singers had now also emerged who were in demand all over the world to sing the principal roles: Anthony Rolfe Johnson and Gösta Winbergh as Idomeneo, Sylvia McNair and Rebecca Evans as Ilia and Carol Vaness as Elettra all appeared in major productions during the 1990s.

The 1990s also saw a number of other important *Idomeneos* that extended the ways in which the opera was explored on stage. David Alden directed an extremely physical production in 1992 in Tel Aviv, as did Andreas Homoki in Munich in 1996, both emphasizing the extreme violence of the characters' emotional lives. Also in 1996, David McVicar at Scottish Opera directed and designed his own first *Idomeneo*. McVicar revealed an immediate and close affinity with eighteenth-century opera and this work in particular. On a limited budget and on a largely bare stage, the characters, including Tom Randle as Idomeneo, Lisa Milne as Ilia, Toby Spence as Idamante and Claire Rutter as Elettra, emerged as particularly clearly defined individuals involved in unusually intense relationships with each other and their world. McVicar revisited the work in a production for Flanders Opera in Ghent three years later, this time designed by Michael Vale in a series of simple painted screens. His cast this time included Richard Croft as Idomeneo and Magdalena Kožená as Idamante, with the early music specialist Marc Minkowski conducting.

Interesting, and even controversial, new productions continued to appear. One of these was in 2003, directed by Hans Neuenfels and designed by Reinhard von der Thannen for the Deutsche Oper, Berlin. The production took a strong anti-religious line, with its protagonists eventually freeing themselves from an oppressive and unfeeling deity. At the end of the final scene, Idomeneo brought on the severed heads of not only Neptune, but also of Christ, the Buddha and Mohammed, leaving them covered in blood on chairs along the front of the stage. A revival was planned for 2006, but threats from Muslim fundamentalists led to it being withdrawn. There was considerable outcry in Germany and beyond about self-censorship on the part of the opera house's administration, and the revival duly went ahead three months later than planned with heightened security measures. No violence occurred.

Another, and arguably less successful, attempt to rethink the opera came in 2003 at Glyndebourne in a collaboration between the director Peter Sellars, the artist Anish Kapoor as designer, the choreographer Mark Morris and conductor Simon Rattle. The performance was extremely long, using a largely uncut 1781 edition, including the full ballet music. Kapoor's at times restricting set and the frequent presence of dancers to shadow the principal singers hampered Sellars in his attempt to make a by now perhaps over-familiar contemporary point about repressive political regimes and the horrors of war. More modest, and certainly shorter, was a production earlier in 2003 by Tim Albery for Opera North in which the action was played out more effectively within a clinical white-tiled set.

As costs rose steadily in the new millennium, opera companies began to share new productions. New shared stagings of *Idomeneo* in the 2000s included those directed by Ursel and Karl-Ernst Herrmann, seen first in Baden-Baden and then in Salzburg and Amsterdam, and by Luc Bondy in Milan, Madrid and Paris. Interest in even the more recondite aspects of the opera continued apace. As an addendum to its performances of all twenty-two of Mozart's operas during the Mozart Year of 2006 to celebrate the 250th anniversary of his birth, the Salzburg Festival gave two concert performances of Richard Strauss's 1931 arrangement, conducted by Fabio Luisi and with Robert Gambill as Idomeneo. A staged production of the Strauss version, an even greater rarity, was given in the Palazzo Ducale as part of the Martina Franca Festival the same year.

There was still more to come. In 2008, Birmingham Opera Company presented a version in English called *King Idomeneo* in a recently vacated rubber factory in Ladywood. The production was directed by Graham Vick and used 2,500 tonnes of especially brought-in earth and 180 amateur local performers, who were involved in both singing and non-singing roles. Audiences were moved from scene to scene in the warehouse-like space and caught up in the action of the opera at close quarters. The same year also saw a production by Opera Atelier in Toronto, which featured, for the first time recorded anywhere, a male soprano, Michael Maniaci, as Idamante. That year the Bayerische Staatsoper also completed its restoration of the Cuvilliés-Theater in Munich, where *Idomeneo* had received its premiere in 1781. On 14th June 2008 Mozart's opera returned home after 227 years, albeit with a tenor Idamante and to a slightly different site within the Residenz building, and was given a special series of performances.

Idomeneo has now taken its place in the international operatic repertory, and is seen and heard all over the world on a regular basis. A large number of recordings in different editions and employing various musical styles is available on CD. DVDs of staged performances of both traditional and more modern productions are also appearing with increasing frequency as opera houses have more of their own productions filmed for presentation to a wider public, initially on television and then commercially. So long neglected, this astonishing achievement of Mozart's early adulthood now seems assuredly recognized as the work of genius that it is.

The Composition of *Idomeneo* in Mozart's Letters

Mozart was twenty-four years old and living in Salzburg with his father Leopold and sister Nannerl when he was commissioned by the Munich court to compose Idomeneo *for performances to take place at the Cuvilliés-Theater in January 1781. The librettist was Abbate Giambattista Varesco, the court chaplain in Salzburg. Mozart began working with him on the opera in Salzburg, but left for Munich on 5th November 1780 to complete the music and begin supervising the singers and musicians for the first performances. Leopold remained in Salzburg and acted as an intermediary between Mozart and Varesco as rehearsals progressed. The series of letters that were exchanged between father and son over the following months leading up to the premiere provide a unique insight into the composition of the opera. What follow are excerpts from some of these.*

Mozart to his father, 8th November 1780, Munich
We didn't arrive until 1 in the afternoon but by evening I'd already been to see Count Seeau.[1] As for the libretto, the count says it's not necessary for Abbate Varesco to copy it out again before sending it here – it's being printed here – but *I* think he should write it out straight away and not forget the *stage directions* and send it here as soon as possible, together with the synopsis. As for the names of the singers, this is the least of our worries, as these can easily be added here. Some small changes will have to be made here and there – the recitatives need shortening a little – but it will *all be printed*.

---

1. Josef Anton, Count Seeau, director of opera and drama at the Munich court.

I've a request to make of the Abbate – Ilia's aria in the second scene of Act Two I'd like to change a little in order to bring it into line with what I need – 'Se il padre perdei, in te lo ritrovo': this couldn't be better – but then comes something that has always struck me as unnatural – I mean in an aria – namely, *an aside*. In a dialogue these things are entirely natural – a few words are hurriedly spoken as an aside – but in an aria, where the words have to be repeated, it creates a bad impression – and even if this weren't the case, I'd still prefer an aria here – if he's happy with it, the opening can stay as it is, as it's delightful – an aria that flows along in an entirely natural way – where I'm not tied to the words but can just let the music continue to flow. [...]

Now for something disagreeable: although I've not had the honour of meeting the hero dal Prato,[2] it seems from the description I've been given of him that Ceccarelli[3] is almost to be preferred. He often runs out of breath in the middle of an aria and – would you believe it? – he's never appeared on stage. Also, Raaff[4] is like a statue, so you can imagine their scene in the opening act.

But now for something good. Madame Dorothea Wendling[5] is *arcicontentissima* with her *scena*. She wanted to hear it three times in succession.

Leopold Mozart to his son, 11th November 1780, Salzburg
I'm returning the libretto and the draft so that His Excellency Count Seeau can see that everything has been done as instructed. A complete copy of the libretto will follow by mail coach in a week's time and will show exactly how Abbate Varesco wants it printed: it will also include the necessary notes.

Here, too, is the aria: I think it's what's needed. If not, let me know as soon as possible. [...] What you say about the singers is depressing, so your music will have to make up for this. You can readily imagine with what childish delight I'm looking forward to hearing the excellent orchestra. I wish I could get away sooner.

---

2. Vincenzo dal Prato, castrato, sang the role of Idamante.
3. Francesco Ceccarelli, castrato at Salzburg Cathedral.
4. Anton Raaff, tenor, sang the role of Idomeneo.
5. Dorothea Wendling, soprano, sang the role of Ilia.

Mozart to his father, 13th November 1780, Munich
To Act One, Scene VIII Quaglio[6] has raised the same objection that
we ourselves made at the very beginning, namely, that it isn't right
that the king should be all on his own on board ship. If the Abbate
thinks that he can be reasonably represented in a terrible storm,
abandoned by everyone, *without a ship*, completely alone and
exposed to the greatest danger, then so be it, but please cut the ship,
as he can't be alone on board a ship – otherwise a few generals who
are in his confidence must disembark with him, but then the king
must say a few words to his men, namely, that they should leave him
on his own, a desire that is entirely natural in the sad situation in
which he finds himself.

Mozart to his father, 15th November 1780, Munich
The aria[7] is excellent as it is – but there's now a further change, for
which Raaff is to blame – but he's right – and even if he weren't, one
would still have to do something to acknowledge his grey hairs. He
was here yesterday – I ran through his first aria with him and he was
very pleased with it; well – the man is old [he was sixty-six]; in an
aria like the one in the second act, 'Fuor del mar ho un mare in seno'
etc., he can no longer show off his abilities – and so, because he has
no aria in the third act and because his aria in the first act can't be
cantabile enough for him as a result of the expression of the words,
he wanted to replace the quartet with a nice aria following his final
speech: 'O Creta fortunata! O me felice!' In this way another useless
number will be cut here – and the third act will now be far more
effective. Now – in the final scene of Act Two – Idomeneo has an
aria or, rather, a kind of cavatina between the choruses – it'll be
better to have just a recitative here, with the instruments working
hard beneath it, for in this scene, which – because of the action and
the grouping, which we've recently agreed on with Le Grand [the
ballet-master] – will be the finest in the whole opera, there'll be so
much noise and confusion on stage that an aria would cut a poor
figure – also, there's the thunderstorm, which I don't suppose will
stop for Herr Raaff's aria, will it? – And the effect of a recitative

---

6. Lorenzo Quaglio, stage designer of *Idomeneo*.
7. 'Se il padre perdei'.

between the choruses is incomparably better. Lisel Wendling[8] has already sung through her two arias half a dozen times – she's very pleased. I have it from a third party that the 2 Wendlings have praised their arias very highly. Raaff is in any case my best and dearest friend!

But I have to go through the whole opera with my *molto amato* castrato dal Prato. He's incapable of singing a meaningful cadenza in an aria, and his voice is uneven! – He's been engaged for only a year and as soon as this period is over, which will be next September, Count Seeau will take on someone else. Ceccarelli could then try his luck. *Sérieusement* –

Leopold Mozart to his son, 18th November 1780, Salzburg
Idomeneo must disembark with his retinue. There follow the words that he addresses to his retinue, who then withdraw. You know that I told Munich of this objection but that they wrote back to say that thunderstorms and seas pay no heed to the laws of *etiquette*. Yes, indeed, if a shipwreck had actually occurred! But the vow spares them. Besides, this landing will produce a splendid impression.

For a long time Varesco was unwilling to make a start on the duet 'Deh soffri in pace o cara' etc., but I've persuaded him to do so. Ilia and Idamante still have a very short argument conducted in a few words of recitative interrupted, *as it were*, by a subterranean noise, after which the oracle is proclaimed by a subterranean voice, which voice and *its accompaniment* must be moving, terrifying and exceptional; it can be a masterpiece of harmony. You'll find enclosed the alteration that has been made.

No. 5 [i.e., the fifth of the changes submitted by Varesco] is the recitative that replaces the duet, the end of which should be declaimed in a very lively manner while she [Ilia] is running to the altar and he [Idamante] holds her back. She then turns to the Priest with great passion and throws herself on her knees, but just as she reaches the words 'A te sacro ministro', the subterranean rumbling prevents her from saying anything more and fills everyone with astonishment and fear. If this is done properly, with one peal of thunder following another, it will produce a great impression on the

8. Elisabeth Augusta Wendling, soprano, sang the role of Elettra.

audience, especially if the subterranean voice is heard immediately afterwards. All this is completely unexpected for the audience and extremely striking and surprising.

Mozart to his father, 29th November 1780, Munich
Tell me, don't you think that the speech of the subterranean voice is too long? Consider it carefully. Imagine the theatre: the voice must be terrifying, it must be penetrating, people must believe that it really exists – how can it achieve this if the speech is too long and the audience is increasingly convinced that it means nothing? If the Ghost's speech in *Hamlet* weren't so long, it would be even more effective. This speech here can easily be shortened and will gain more than it loses in the process.

Mozart to his father, 1st December 1780, Munich
The rehearsal passed off exceptionally well. There were only six violins in total, but all the necessary wind instruments. No audience was admitted except for Count Seeau's sister and young Count Sensheim. We'll have another rehearsal in a week's time, when we'll have twelve violinists for the first act, which in the meantime I'm having copied for twice as many players, and we'll also be rehearsing the second act, just as we rehearsed the first act last time. I can't tell you how delighted and astonished they all were.

Leopold Mozart to his son, 4th December 1780, Salzburg
You know that *I too thought the subterranean speech too long.* I've told him [Varesco] my honest opinion, and it will now be as short as possible. We are delighted to hear that the rehearsal went so well. I have no doubt whatsoever nor am I anxious about your work as long as the production is good, in other words, *as long as there are good people to perform it* – and there are. And so I'm not worried. But your music will always lose out when it's performed by a mediocre orchestra because it is so well written for all the instruments and isn't as plain as Italian music generally is.

Mozart to his father, 5 December 1780, Munich
As for Raaff's final aria, I said that we both wanted something more pleasing, something more agreeably worded – the word 'era' is forced. The opening would do at a pinch, but 'gelida massa' is again problematical. In short, arcane or unusual words are always unsuited to an aria that ought to be pleasing.

Also, I'd like the aria to express only peace and contentment – even if it were only in *one section* – that would be all right, indeed I'd almost prefer it. I also told you about Panzacchi[9] – we must do what we can to oblige this honest old man. He'd like his recitative in Act Three to be a couple of lines longer – because he's a good actor and because of the chiaro e oscuro, this will create a fine impression. For example, after the verse 'Sei la città del pianto, e questa reggia quella del duol' ['You are the city of tears, and this kingdom is the kingdom of grief'], there is a brief glimmer of hope – and then! – 'What a fool I am! How my anguish has misled me! Ah Creta tutta io vedo etc.'

But Abbate Varesco doesn't need to write out the whole act all over again on account of these changes – they can easily be added. I also said that both I and others think that the subterranean speech seems too long to be effective. Just think it over.

Leopold Mozart to his son, 11th December 1780, Salzburg
I am enclosing a note from Varesco and also the aria. I expect that the *first act, together with the translation*, and perhaps also the *second* act will reach you *in Munich* by mail coach next week. I hope you're keeping well.

I advise you when working on the score to consider not only the musical but also the *unmusical public*. You know that for every *10 real connoisseurs* there are *100 ignoramuses*. So don't forget what's called the *popular* style, which tickles long ears.

Leopold Mozart to his son, 15th December 1780, Salzburg
Herr Fiala[10] has just dropped by and shown me a letter from Herr Becke,[11] which was full of praise for your music for the first act:

---

9. Domenico de' Panzacchi, tenor, sang the role of Arbace
10. Joseph Fiala, composer, cellist and viol player.
11. Johann Baptist Becke, flautist in the Munich court chapel and a family friend.

he wrote that *tears* of joy and delight *came to his eyes* when he heard this music and that everyone maintained that *it was the most beautiful music they had ever heard, that it was all new and strange etc., that they were now about to rehearse the second act, that he would then write to me in person, and that I should forgive him for not having written before, but he's been a little out of sorts etc.* Well, thank God, everything's going well. *I know your work,* and so I can't believe that these are empty compliments. No, I'm convinced that if your work is adequately performed, it is bound to be effective.

Mozart to his father, 16th December 1780, Munich
As for what is called popular taste, don't worry, for my opera contains music for all kinds of people, not just for those with long ears.

Mozart to his father, 19th December 1780, Munich
The last rehearsal, like the first, turned out very well. The orchestra and the whole audience discovered to their delight that they'd been wrong in thinking that the second act couldn't possibly be more powerful than the first in terms of its expression and originality [...]

That I'm well, and contented, you'll have noticed from my letters. After all, who wouldn't be happy to be finally rid of such a great and glorious task – and to be rid, moreover, with honour and fame – for I've nearly finished. All that's missing are 3 arias and the final chorus from Act Three, the Overture and the ballet. And then, *adieu partie*! [...]

The scene between father and son in the first scene in Act One – and the first scene in Act Two between Idomeneo and Arbace – are both too long – they'll undoubtedly bore people, especially as in the first scene both the singers are bad actors – and in the second scene, one of them is – and their entire content is no more than a recital of what the audience has already seen with its own eyes. These scenes will be printed as they stand, but I'd like the Abbate to show me how they can be cut and made as short as possible. Otherwise I'll have to cut them myself, as these two scenes can't remain as they are – I mean, when set to music.

Leopold Mozart to his son, 22nd December 1780, Salzburg
You're absolutely insistent on shortening 2 recitatives. I sent for Varesco at once as I didn't receive your letter till 5 o'clock in the evening and the mail coach leaves early tomorrow morning. We've examined it from every point of view and can find no reason to shorten it. It's translated from the French, as the draft envisaged. Indeed, if you look at the draft, you'll see that it was demanded that this recitative should be lengthened a little so that they [Idomeneo and Idamante in Act One, Scene X] don't recognize each other too quickly and now there's the risk that it'll be made to seem ridiculous if they recognize each other after only a few words. [...] Or do you want father and son to run into each other the way that the disguised Harlequin and Brighella meet as servants in a foreign country and quickly recognize and embrace each other? Remember that this is one *of the most beautiful scenes in the opera*, indeed, it's the main scene and the one on which the whole of the rest of the story depends. In any case, this scene can't weary the audience *as it's in the first act.*

Mozart to his father, 27th December 1780, Munich
As for the two scenes that are to be shortened, this wasn't my suggestion, merely something to which I consented, my reason being that Raaff and dal Prato sing the recitative entirely without spirit and fire and in a completely monotonous way – and they're the most pitiful actors ever to set foot on a stage. I had a terrible row the other day with Seeau about the impropriety, unnaturalness and virtual impossibility of omitting anything. It's enough that everything is printed as it stands – which, initially at least, he absolutely refused to accept – but he finally agreed to it after I'd really laid in to him. The last rehearsal passed off splendidly. It took place in a large room at court; the elector was also present – this time we had the whole orchestra – I mean as many players as there is room for in the opera house.

After the first act, the elector called out to me in a very loud voice, shouting 'Bravo', and when I went over to him to kiss his hand, he said: *'This opera will be charming; it cannot fail to do you honour.'*

Leopold Mozart to his son, 29th December 1780, Salzburg
I assume that you'll use deep wind instruments to accompany the subterranean voice. How would it be if after the *vague* subterranean noise the instruments were to *sustain* their notes or, *rather, begin to sustain them piano*, followed by a *crescendo that adds to the element of terror*, with the *voice entering at the decrescendo* and with another terrifying *crescendo each time the voice falls silent*? The noise, which must be brief and like the shock of an earthquake, causing the statue of Neptune to move, captures everyone's attention, and this attention is increased by the entry of a quiet and sustained passage for winds that grows louder and louder and instils a sense of extreme terror, building to a climax, at which point *a single voice* is heard – I can already hear and see it in my imagination.

Mozart to his father, 30th December 1780, Munich
Happy New Year! – Forgive me for writing so little on this occasion, but I'm up to my eyes in work – I've not quite finished the third act, and as there's no ballet but only an appropriate divertissement, I've the honour of writing the music for this too. But I'm very pleased that this is so, because it means that all the music will be by the same composer. The third act will be *at least* as good as the other two – in fact I think it will be infinitely better and that people will be able to say with some truth: *Finis coronat opus.*

Mozart to his father, 3rd January 1781, Munich
My head and hands are so full of the third act that it wouldn't surprise me if I turned into a third act myself. This act alone has given me more trouble than a whole opera – there's hardly a scene in it that isn't extremely interesting. The accompaniment to the subterranean voice consists of only 5 voices, namely, 3 trombones and 2 horns, which are positioned in the same place as the voice. The whole orchestra is silent at this point –

The dress rehearsal will *definitely* be on the 20th – and the first performance on the 22nd.

Mozart to his father, 10th/11th January 1781, Munich
The latest news is that the opera has again been postponed for a week – the dress rehearsal will now take place on the 27th – my birthday

– and the first performance on the 29th – why? – presumably so that Count Seeau can save a few hundred florins. But I'm pleased, as it means that we can have more rehearsals. [...] Next Saturday we'll be rehearsing all 3 acts in the rehearsal room. [...] Forgive me if I write very little this time and if I close now but, first, as you can see, my pen and ink are useless and, 2nd, I still have to write some arias for the ballet.

Mozart to his father, 18th January 1781, Munich
Please forgive me if on this occasion I write very little but I have to leave for the rehearsal this very moment: it's almost 10 – in the morning, I mean. This is the first time we've rehearsed the recitatives in the theatre; – I haven't been able to write till now because I was still working on these confounded dances – God be praised – I've survived. For now, let me tell you only the most important news: the rehearsal of the third act turned out splendidly. People thought it much better than the first 2 acts. But the libretto is too long, and so the music is too – I've always said as much. As a result, Idamante's aria, 'No, la morte io non pavento', is to be omitted – it was in any case out of place here. But the people who've heard the music to it regret this decision. Raaff's final aria is also being cut, something that people regret even more – but – we must make a virtue of necessity. The pronouncement of the oracle is also far too long – I've made it shorter – Varesco doesn't need to know about all this as it will be printed just as he wrote it.

Thematic Guide

Devised by Julian Rushton

Themes from the opera have been identified by the numbers in square brackets in the article on the music. These are also printed at corresponding points in the libretto, so that the words can be related to the musical themes.

[2] IDAMANTE

Non ho col - pa, e mi con - dan - ni, e mi con - dan - ni

[3]

Allegro con brio

Go - diam la pa - ce, tri - on - fi A - mo - re, A - mo - re

[4] ELETTRA

Allegro assai

Tut - te nel cor vi sen - to, vi sen - to, vi

sen - to, fu - rie del cru - do a - ver - no,

[5]

[Allegro assai]

CHORUS on shore (echoed by chorus of sailors)

p *cresc.* Pie - tà! Nu - mi, pie - tà!

[6a] IDOMENEO

Andantino sostenuto

Ve - drom - mi in - tor - no l'om - bra do - len - te,

[6b]

Allegro di molto

Qual spa - ven - to, qual do - lo - re, qual spa - ven - to, quall do - lo - re!

[7] IDAMANTE

Allegro

[violins]

Il pa - dre a do - ra - to ri - tro - vo, e lo per - do.

[8] Marcia

f

[9] Ciaccona

p *cresc.* Net - tu - no s'o - no - ri

[10a] ARBACE

Allegro

Se il tuo duol, se il mio de - si - o

[10b] Rondò (1786)
Andante
Solo violin

IDAMANTE (tenor)

Non te - mer, a - ma - to___ be - ne,

[11a] ILIA
Andante ma sostenuto

Se il pa - dre per - de - i, la pa-tria il ri - po-so, tu pa - dre___ mi___ se - i,

[11b] (Flute, oboe)

[12a] Andante
In tempo dell'Aria
IDAMANTE

Muted strings
Qual mi con-tur-ba i sen-si e-qui-vo-ca fa - vel- la?

[13] ELETTRA
Recitativo

I - dol mi - o, se ri - tro-so al - tro a - man-te a me___ ti___ ren- de,

[14] Marcia

p assai

[15] CHORUS
Andantino

Pla - ci-do è il mar, an - dia - mo, tut - to ci ras - si - cu - ra,

[16] IDAMANTE
Andante

Pria___ di par - tir, oh___ Di - o! sof - fri che un ba-cio im - pri - ma

55

[29] Allegro assai

p   cresc.   f

ELETTRA

D'O - re - ste, d'A - ia - ce

[30a] Adagio

p   3

p

[30b] IDOMENEO

Adagio

Tor - na la pa - ce al co - re, al co - re

[31] Allegro vivace

(violins)

Scen - da A - mor, scen - da I - me - ne - o

[32] Chaconne (Allegro)

f

60

Idomeneo, re di Creta

Dramma per musica in three acts
by Wolfgang Amadeus Mozart (K366)

Libretto by Giambattista Varesco
English translation by Charles Johnston

Idomeneo was first performed at the Cuvilliés-Theater, Munich, on 29th January 1781. The first professional performance in Britain was at Glyndebourne on 20th June 1951. The first professional performance in the United States was at Tanglewood on 4th August 1947.

THE CHARACTERS

Idomeneo *King of Crete*	tenor
Idamante *his son*	soprano or tenor
Ilia *a Trojan princess*	soprano
Elettra *a Greek princess*	soprano
Arbace *confidant of Idomeneo*	tenor
High Priest of Neptune	tenor
Voice of Neptune	bass

Trojan prisoners; sailors; people of Crete

The action is set in Mycenaean Crete following the end of the Trojan War.

Translator's Note

Charles Johnston

This translation aims to make available in modern English prose, perhaps for the first time in a single volume, all the text Mozart set to music for *Idomeneo*, along with the relevant stage directions. What follows thus disregards any specific 'version' of the libretto actually given by Mozart or by opera companies or recordings since his death; indeed, any attempt to perform the complete text translated here would be pointless, as it incorporates the new compositions for the Vienna performance of 1786 (Nos. 10b and 20b) and thus includes two different opening scenes to Act Two and two different duets for Ilia and Idamante in Act Three, Scene II. Since the Vienna numbers were wholesale replacements of their 1781 equivalents, with no new simple recitative added, it has been possible to insert them (differentiated by a light grey background) within the complete sequence, which otherwise gives all the text Mozart set for Munich. We have not attempted to indicate omissions of arias or internal cuts within simple or accompanied recitative which are known to have been made for specific performances: hence we print, for instance, the longest text of the recitative for The Voice [28], which exists in four distinct versions, and of Elettra's accompanied recitative that comes shortly afterwards (Mozart cut some lines from this when he rewrote it and omitted her aria, No. 29. The only sections of Varesco's libretto not translated here are those that, as far is known, the composer never set to music, such as the additional strophes for Elettra's Act Two aria, Idomeneo's 'Torna la pace' in Act Three and the final chorus.

The libretto is here reproduced in modernized Italian. Although it has frequently been printed as prose, notably by record companies keen to save space, Varesco's recitative is written in verse lines of seven or eleven syllables, with speeches often rounded off by rhyming couplets. This layout has been preserved here, and the translation endeavours to follow the sequence and literal meaning of the Italian as far as is compatible with a comprehensible English version. No claim is made to literary merit.

Endnotes on p. 156, indicated in the translation by asterisks, explain all but the most obvious classical references. Proper names except those of the dramatis personae are given in the normal English form of their Latin version, even though the action takes place in Homeric Crete where Neptune would have been known as Poseidon, Jupiter as Zeus, and so forth; this conforms to Varesco's Italianate usage. However, the names of the opera's characters have been left in Italian: aside from Idomeneo and Elettra, none of them appears in classical sources, and Electra the unfortunate daughter of Agamemnon and brother of Orestes (both mentioned in the libretto) is never connected with King Idomeneus by the ancient writers.

This translation is based on the one originally commissioned by Harmonia Mundi France in 2008 to accompany René Jacobs's recording of the Munich version. It has been thoroughly revised, and expanded to include the two Vienna numbers and a few short passages of recitative not recorded by HM. The translator would like to thank Julian Rushton for his advice on textual matters during the process of revision.

Ouverture [0a, 0b, 0c, 0d]

ATTO PRIMO

Appartamenti d'Ilia nel palazzo reale, in fondo al prospetto una galleria.

Scena I

Ilia sola

ILIA

Quando avran fine omai
l'aspre sventure mie? Ilia infelice,
di tempesta crudel misero avanzo,
del genitor e de' germani priva,
del barbaro nemico
misto col sangue il sangue
vittime generose,
a qual sorte più rea
ti riserbano i Numi?...
Pur vendicaste voi
di Priamo e di Troia i danni e l'onte?
Perì la flotta argiva, e Idomeneo
pasto forse sarà d'orca vorace...
Ma che mi giova, oh ciel! se al primo aspetto
di quel prode Idamante,
che all'onde mi rapì, l'odio deposi,
e pria fu schiavo il cor che m'accorgessi
d'essere prigioniera?
Ah qual contrasto, oh Dio! d'opposti affetti
mi destate nel sen, odio ed amore!
Vendetta deggio a chi mi diè la vita,
gratitudine a chi vita mi rende...

64

Overture [0a, 0b, 0c, 0d]

ACT ONE

Ilia's apartments in the royal palace; in the background, an arcade.

Scene I

Ilia alone

ILIA

When will my bitter misfortunes
at last come to an end? Unhappy Ilia,
wretched survivor of a cruel storm,
deprived of your father and brothers,
those generous victims
whose blood mingled with the blood
of the savage foe,
what still more evil fate
do the gods have in store for you?
Were you not avenged, O gods,
by the ruin and shame of Priam and Troy?
The Greek fleet has perished, and Idomeneo
is perhaps the prey of a voracious sea-beast...
But what matter, oh Heaven, when at my first sight
of brave Idamante,
who saved me from the waves, I set aside my hate,
and my heart was enslaved before I realized
that I was a prisoner.
Oh God, what a conflict of contrary emotions
have you roused in my heart: hate and love!
I owe vengeance to him who gave me life,
and gratitude to him who restored life to me...

Oh Ilia! oh genitor! oh prence! oh sorte!
Oh vita sventurata! oh dolce morte!
Ma che? m'ama Idamante?... ah no; l'ingrato
per Elettra sospira, e quella Elettra,
meschina principessa esule d'Argo,
d'Oreste alle sciagure a queste arene
fuggitiva, raminga, è mia rivale.
Quanti mi siete intorno
carnefici spietati?... orsù sbranate,
vendetta, gelosia, odio ed amore,
sbranate sì quest'infelice core!

N°1 Aria

Padre, germani, addio!   [1a]
  voi foste, io vi perdei.
  Grecia, cagion tu sei.
  E un Greco adorerò?
D'ingrata al sangue mio   [1b]
  so che la colpa avrei;
  ma quel sembiante, oh Dei!
  odiare ancor non so.

Ecco Idamante, ahimè!
sen vien. Misero core,
tu palpiti e paventi.
Deh cessate per poco, oh miei tormenti!

Scena II

Idamante, Ilia; seguito d'Idamante

IDAMANTE *(al seguito)*
Radunate i Troiani, ite, e la corte
sia pronta questo giorno a celebrar.
(a Ilia) Di dolce speme a un raggio
scema il mio duol. Minerva, della Grecia
protettrice, involò al furor dell'onde
il padre mio. In mar di qui non lunge
comparser le sue navi. Indaga Arbace
il sito che a noi toglie
l'augusto aspetto.

Oh, Ilia! Oh, father! Oh, prince! Oh, fate!
Oh, life of misfortune! Oh, sweet death!
What then? Does Idamante love me? But no.
The ingrate sighs for Elettra, and Elettra,
that poor exiled princess from Argos,
who came to these shores to flee
the misfortunes of Orestes,* is my rival.
How many of you are there around me,
pitiless torturers? Come, tear me to pieces,
vengeance, jealousy, hate and love,
tear this unhappy heart to pieces!

No. 1 Aria

Father, brothers, farewell! [1a]
　You are no more; I have lost you.
　Greece, you are the cause of this;
　and should I now adore a Greek?
I know I would be guilty [1b]
　if I denied my own kin.
　But that countenance, oh gods!
　I still cannot bring myself to hate it.

Here is Idamante, alas!
He is approaching. My poor heart,
you flutter and are afraid.
Ah, cease but for a moment, my torments!

Scene II

Idamante, Ilia; retinue of Idamante

IDAMANTE *(to his retinue)*
　Assemble the Trojans; go now, and let the court
　prepare to celebrate this day.
　(to Ilia) A ray of sweet hope
　lessens my torment. Minerva, protectress
　of Greece, has saved my father
　from the fury of the waves. His fleet has been seen
　at sea, not far from here. Arbace is searching for
　the spot which still deprives us
　of his august countenance.

ILIA *(con ironia)*

Non temer: difesa
da Minerva è la Grecia, e tutta ormai
scoppiò sovra i Troian l'ira de' Numi.

IDAMANTE

Del fato de' Troian più non dolerti.
Farà il figlio per lor quanto farebbe
il genitor e ogn'altro
vincitor generoso. Ecco: abbian fine,
principessa, i lor guai:
rendo lor libertade, e omai fra noi
sol prigioniero fia, sol fia che porte
chi tua beltà legò care ritorte.

ILIA

Signor, che ascolto? Non saziaro ancora
d'implacabili Dei l'odio, lo sdegno
d'Ilion le gloriose
or diroccate mura, ah non più mura,
ma vasto, e piano suol? A eterno pianto
dannate son le nostre egre pupille?

IDAMANTE

Venere noi punì, di noi trionfa.
Quanto il mio genitor, ahi rimembranza!
soffrì de' flutti in sen? Agamennone
vittima in Argo al fin, a caro prezzo
comprò que' suoi trofei, e non contenta
di tante stragi ancor la Dea nemica,
che fè? Il mio cor trafisse,
Ilia, co' tuoi bei lumi
più possenti de' suoi,
e in me vendica adesso i danni tuoi.

ILIA

Che dici?

IDAMANTE

Sì, di Citerea il figlio
incogniti tormenti
stillommi in petto. A te pianto e scompiglio

ILIA *(with irony)*

Have no fear: Greece
is defended by Minerva, and all the anger
of the gods has already burst on the Trojans.

IDAMANTE

Grieve no more over the Trojans' fate.
The son will do for them as would
the father and any other
generous victor. Behold: let their woes
come to an end, princess;
I restore their freedom. Among us now
may there be only one prisoner: he who bears
the sweet chains in which your beauty has bound him.

ILIA

Lord, what do I hear? Are the hatred and anger
of the implacable gods still not satisfied
by the demolition of the once glorious
walls of Ilium* – walls no longer,
but a vast razed plain? Are our poor eyes
condemned to eternal weeping?

IDAMANTE

Venus has punished us, and triumphs over us.
How much did my father (ah, bitter memory!)
suffer amid the waves? In the end Agamemnon,
a victim in Argos, paid a high price
for his trophies. And, still not content
with such slaughter, what did the hostile goddess do?
She pierced my heart,
Ilia, with your lovely eyes,
more potent than hers,
and now avenges your wrongs on me.

ILIA

What are you saying?

IDAMANTE

Yes, Cytherea's son*
has instilled unknown torments
in my breast. Mars has brought you

69

Marte portò, cercò vendetta Amore
in me de' mali tuoi, quei vaghi rai,
quei tuoi vezzi adoprò… Ma all'amor mio
d'ira e rossor tu avvampi?

ILIA

In questi accenti
mal soffro un temerario ardir. Deh pensa,
pensa Idamante, oh Dio!
il padre tuo qual è, qual era il mio.

N°2 *Aria*

IDAMANTE

Non ho colpa, e mi condanni,   [2]
  idol mio, perché t'adoro.
  Colpa è vostra, o Dei tiranni,
  e di pena afflitto io moro
  d'un error che mio non è.
Se tu il brami, al tuo impero   [0c]
  aprirommi questo seno.
  Ne' tuoi lumi il leggo, è vero,
  ma mel dica il labbro almeno,
  e non chiedo altra mercé.

ILIA *(vede condurre i prigionieri)*
Ecco il misero resto de' Troiani,
dal nemico furor salvi.

IDAMANTE

Or quei ceppi
io romperò, vuo' consolarli adesso.
(da sé) Ahi! perché tanto far non so a me stesso!

Scena III

Idamante, Ilia.
Troiani prigionieri, uomini e donne cretesi

IDAMANTE *(si levano a' prigionieri le catene, li quali dimostrano gratitudine)*
Scingete le catene, ed oggi il mondo,
oh fedele Sidon suddita nostra,

tears and agitation; Love has sought vengeance
for your sufferings in me, employing
your fair eyes, your charms... But you burn
with anger and shame at my love?

ILIA

                                 I take ill
the bold ardour of these words. Pray think,
think, Idamante, oh God,
who is your father, and who was mine.

No. 2 Aria

IDAMANTE
   I am blameless, and you condemn me,   [2]
      my idol, because I adore you.
      The fault is yours, O tyrannous gods,
      and I die afflicted with distress
      for a crime that is not mine.
   If you so wish, at your command,   [0c]
      I will pierce this breast of mine.
      I read it in your eyes, it is true,
      but at least let your lips tell me so,
      and I ask no other favour.

ILIA *(seeing the prisoners brought in)*
   Here are the pitiful remnants of the Trojans
   who escaped the enemy's fury.

IDAMANTE
                           I will break
their chains; now I wish to console them.
(Aside) Ah! If only I could do the same for myself!

Scene III

Idamante, Ilia.
Trojan prisoners, Cretan men and women

IDAMANTE *(the prisoners are freed of their chains, and show
their gratitude)*
   Unlock the chains, and today,
   O faithful subject city of Cydonia,*

vegga due gloriosi
popoli in dolce nodo avvinti e stretti
di perfetta amistà.
Elena armò la Grecia e l'Asia, ed ora
disarma e riunisce ed Asia e Grecia,
eroina novella,
principessa più amabile, e più bella.

N°3 Coro

Coro de' Troiani e Cretesi

TUTTI
  Godiam la pace,   [3]
    trionfi Amore:
    ora ogni core
    giubilerà.

DUE CRETESI
  Grazie a chi estinse
    face di guerra:
    or sì la terra
    riposo avrà.

TUTTI
  Godiam la pace,
    trionfi Amore:
    ora ogni core
    giubilerà.

DUE TROIANI
  A voi dobbiamo,
    pietosi Numi,
    e a' quei bei lumi
    la libertà.

TUTTI
  Godiam la pace,
    trionfi Amore:
    ora ogni core
    giubilerà.

let the world see two glorious peoples
bound by a sweet knot and linked
by perfect friendship.
Helen armed Greece and Asia, and now
a new heroine,
a princess more kindly and more beautiful,
disarms and reunites Asia and Greece.

No. 3 Chorus

Chorus of Trojans and Cretans

ALL
    Let us enjoy peace,   [3]
      let Love triumph:
      now every heart
      will rejoice.

TWO CRETAN WOMEN
    Thanks to him who quenched
      the torch of war:
      now the land
      will find rest.

ALL
    Let us enjoy peace,
      let Love triumph:
      now every heart
      will rejoice.

TWO TROJANS
    To you,
      merciful gods,
      and to those fair eyes,
      we owe our freedom.

ALL
    Let us enjoy peace,
      let Love triumph:
      now every heart
      will rejoice.

Scena IV

Elettra, e detti

ELETTRA *(agitata da gelosia)*
Prence, signor, tutta la Grecia oltraggi;
tu proteggi il nemico.

IDAMANTE
Veder basti alla Grecia
vinto il nemico. Opra di me più degna
a mirar s'apparecchi, oh principessa:
vegga il vinto felice.

(vede venire Arbace)

Arbace viene.

Scena V

Arbace, e detti (Arbace è mesto)

IDAMANTE *(timoroso)*
Ma quel pianto che annunzia?

ARBACE
Mio signore,
de' mali il più terribil...

IDAMANTE *(ansioso)*
Più non vive
il genitor?

ARBACE
Non vive: quel che Marte
far non poté finor, fece Nettuno,
l'inesorabil nume,
e degl'eroi il più degno, ora il riseppi,
presso a straniera sponda
affogato morì!

IDAMANTE
Ilia, de' viventi
eccoti il più meschin. Or sì dal cielo
soddisfatta sarai... barbaro fato!...
Corrasi al lido... ahimè! son disperato! *(parte)*

Scene IV

Elettra, the previous

ELETTRA *(goaded by jealousy)*
    Prince, lord, you outrage all Greece;
    you protect the enemy.

IDAMANTE
    It is enough for Greece to see
    her enemy defeated. Prepare to see
    a deed worthier of me, princess:
    behold the happy vanquished.

(he sees Arbace coming)

                                    Arbace comes.

Scene V

Arbace, the previous (Arbace looks sorrowful)

IDAMANTE *(apprehensively)*
    But what do these tears announce?

ARBACE

                                    My lord,

    the most terrible of woes…

IDAMANTE *(anxiously)*

                            Is my father

    no longer alive?

ARBACE

                        He lives no more. What Mars
    could not do has been accomplished by Neptune,
    that inexorable god:
    the worthiest of heroes, as I have just heard,
    was drowned
    near a foreign shore!

IDAMANTE

                        Ilia, of all men living
    behold the unhappiest. Now you must be
    satisfied with Heaven's deeds. Cruel fate!
    I must run to the shore. Ah, I am desperate! *(exit)*

ILIA

Dell'Asia i danni ancora
troppo risento, e pur d'un grand'eroe
al nome, al caso, il cor parmi commosso,
e negargli i sospir, ah no, non posso.

(parte sospirando)

Scena VI

Elettra sola

ELETTRA

Estinto è Idomeneo?... Tutto a' miei danni,
tutto congiura il ciel. Può a suo talento
Idamante disporre
d'un impero e del cor, e a me non resta
ombra di speme? A mio dispetto, ahi lassa!
vedrò, vedrà la Grecia a suo gran scorno
una schiava troiana di quel soglio
e del talamo a parte... Invano Elettra
ami l'ingrato... E soffre
una figlia d'un re, che ha re vassalli,
che una vil schiava aspiri al grand'acquisto?...
Oh sdegno! oh smanie! oh duol!... più non resisto.

N°4 Aria

Tutte nel cor vi sento, [4]
    furie del crudo Averno,
    lunge a sì gran tormento
    amor, mercé, pietà.
Chi mi rubò quel core,
    quel che tradito ha il mio,
    provin dal mio furore, [0c]
    vendetta e crudeltà. *(parte)*

Scena VII

*Spiagge del mare ancora agitato attorniate da dirupi. Rottami di
navi sul lido. Coro di gente vicina a naufragare*

ILIA

    I still feel too keenly
    the misfortunes of Asia, yet the name and the fate
    of this great hero move my heart,
    and I cannot, no, cannot refuse him my sighs.

(exit, sighing)

Scene VI

Elettra alone

ELETTRA

    Is Idomeneo dead? Then Heaven contrives
    everything for my ruin. Can Idamante
    do as he wishes
    with an empire and his heart, while for me
    not a shred of hope is left? In spite of myself, alas,
    I shall see, and to its shame Greece too will see
    a Trojan slave share his throne
    and his bed... In vain, Elettra,
    you love this ingrate. Must the daughter of a king,
    who has kings as vassals,
    let a vile slave aspire to such great honour?
    Oh rage! Frenzy! Grief! I can resist no longer.

No. 4 Aria

    I feel you all in my heart,   [4]
      Furies of cruel Avernus,*
      insensible to such great torment,
      to love, mercy, and pity.
    Let her who robbed me of his heart,
      and him who betrayed mine,
      feel the vengeance and cruelty   [0c]
      of my rage. *(exit)*

Scene VII

A sea-coast surrounded by rocks, with the waves still agitated. Wreckage from ships on the shore. Chorus of people on the point of shipwreck

N°5 *Coro*

TUTTI *(forte)*
>Pietà Numi, pietà!   [5]
>>Aiuto, o giusti Numi!
>>A noi volgete i lumi...

PARTE DEL CORO *(scemando)*
>Pietà Numi, pietà!
>>Il ciel, il mare, il vento
>>ci opprimon di spavento...

ALTRA PARTE DEL CORO *(piano)*
>Pietà Numi, pietà!
>>In braccio a cruda morte
>>ci spinge l'empia sorte...

TUTTI
>Pietà Numi, pietà.

Scena VIII

Pantomima

Nettuno comparisce sul mare. Fa cenno a' venti di ritirarsi alle loro spelonche. Il mare poco a poco si calma. Idomeneo, vedendo il Dio del mare, implora la sua potenza. Nettuno, riguardandolo con occhio torvo e minaccevole, si tuffa nell'onde e sparisce.
Idomeneo con seguito

Scena IX

IDOMENEO *(al suo seguito)*
>Eccoci salvi alfin. Oh voi, di Marte
>e di Nettuno all'ire,
>alle vittorie, ai stenti
>fidi seguaci miei,
>lasciatemi per poco
>qui solo respirar, e al ciel natìo
>confidar il passato affanno mio.

(Il seguito si ritira, e Idomeneo solo s'inoltra sul lido, contemplando.)

No. 5 *Chorus*

ALL *(loudly)*
    Mercy, O gods, mercy!   [5]
      Help us, just gods!
      Turn your eyes on us...

A SECTION OF THE CHORUS *(less loudly)*
    Mercy, O gods, mercy!
      Sky, sea and wind
      overwhelm us with terror...

ANOTHER SECTION OF THE CHORUS *(softly)*
    Mercy, O gods, mercy!
      Pitiless fate thrusts us
      into the arms of cruel death...

ALL
    Mercy, O gods, mercy!

Scene VIII

Pantomime

Neptune appears on the sea. He signals to the winds to withdraw to their caverns. The sea gradually grows calm. Idomeneo, seeing the god of the sea, implores his might. Neptune, looking at him with grim and threatening gaze, plunges into the waves and vanishes. Idomeneo and his retinue

Scene IX

IDOMENEO *(to his retinue)*
    Now we are safe at last. You who,
    braving the rage of Mars and Neptune,
    have faithfully followed me
    to victories and hardships,
    let me breathe here alone
    for a moment, and tell my native skies
    of my past afflictions.

(His retinue withdraws and Idomeneo continues alone on the shore, lost in contemplation.)

IDOMENEO
Tranquillo è il mar, aura soave spira
di dolce calma, e le cerulee sponde
il biondo Dio indora. Ovunque io miro,
tutto di pace in sen riposa, e gode.
Io sol, io sol su queste aride spiagge,
d'affanno e da disagio estenuato,
quella calma, oh Nettuno, in me non provo,
che al tuo regno impetrai.
In mezzo a' flutti e scogli,
dall'ira tua sedotto, a te lo scampo
dal naufragio chiedei, e in olocausto
il primo de' mortali che qui intorno
infelice s'aggiri, all'are tue
pien di terror promisi. All'empio voto
eccomi in salvo sì, ma non in pace...
Ma son pur quelle, oh Dio! le care mura,
dove la prima io trassi aura vitale?...
Lungi da sì gran tempo, ah con qual core
ora vi rivedrò, se appena in seno
da voi accolto, un misero innocente
dovrò svenar! Oh voto insano, atroce!
Giuramento crudel! Ah qual de' Numi
mi serba ancor in vita,
o qual di voi mi porge almen aita?

N°6 *Aria*

Vedrommi intorno   [6a]
   l'ombra dolente,
   che notte e giorno:
   'Sono innocente'
   m'accennerà.
Nel sen trafitto
   nel corpo esangue
   il mio delitto,
   lo sparso sangue
   m'additerà.
Qual spavento,   [6b]

IDOMENEO

The sea is tranquil, a gentle breeze
blows sweet calm, and the blond god*
gilds the sands by the blue sea. Wherever I look,
all rests in peace and rejoices.
Only I, I alone, on these barren shores,
exhausted by affliction and privations,
do not feel, O Neptune, the calm
that I beseeched in your kingdom.
Amid the waves and reefs,
tempted by your anger, I asked you
to spare me from shipwreck, and, full of terror,
promised as a sacrifice to your altars
the first unfortunate mortal
who would come here. Thanks to that impious vow,
here I am in safety, yes, but not in peace…
But is that the dear city, oh God,
where I first drew breath?…
After such a long absence, how heavy is my heart
to see you once more, if no sooner am I welcomed
within your walls than I must sacrifice
a poor innocent! Oh, insane, dreadful vow!
Cruel oath! Ah, which of the gods
still keeps me alive?
Which of them will come to my aid?

No. 6 Aria

I will see around me   [6a]
   the sorrowing shade
   who, night and day,
   will say to me:
   'I am innocent.'
On his pierced breast,
   on his pallid corpse,
   the blood I have shed
   will show me
   my crime.
What horror,   [6b]

81

qual dolore!
Di tormento
questo core
quante volte morirà!

(Vede un uomo che s'avvicina.)

Cieli! che veggo? Ecco, la sventurata
vittima, ahimè, s'appressa... Oh qual dolore
mostra quel ciglio! Mi si gela il sangue,
fremo d'orror... E vi fia grata, oh Numi,
legittima vi sembra
ostia umana innocente?... E queste mani
le ministre saran?... Mani esecrande!
Barbari, ingiusti Numi! Are nefande!

Scena X

Idomeneo, Idamante (in disparte)

IDAMANTE

Spiagge romite, e voi, scoscese rupi,
testimoni al mio duol siate e cortesi
di questo vostro albergo
a un agitato cor... Quanto spiegate
di mia sorte il rigor, solinghi orrori!...
Vedo fra quegl'avanzi
di fracassate navi su quel lido
sconosciuto guerrier... Voglio ascoltarlo,
vuo' confortarlo e voglio
in letizia cangiar quel suo cordoglio.

(S'appressa e parla a Idomeneo.)

Sgombra, oh guerrier, qual tu ti sia, il timore;
eccoti pronto a tuo soccorso quello
che in questo clima offrir tel può.

IDOMENEO *(da sé)*

                                    Più il guardo,
più mi strugge il dolor. *(a Idamante)* De' giorni miei
il resto a te dovrò. Tu quale avrai
premio da me?

what sorrow!
In its torment,
how many times
this heart will die!

(He sees a man coming.)

Heavens! What do I see? Behold, the unhappy
victim approaches, alas… Oh, what grief
his eyes reveal! My blood freezes,
I shudder with horror. Does this please you,
O gods, does it seem right to you to sacrifice
this innocent human victim? And must my hands
be the agents of his death? Loathsome hands!
Savage, unjust gods! Wicked altars!

Scene X

Idomeneo, Idamante (some way off)

IDAMANTE

Solitary shores and rugged cliffs,
bear witness to my sorrow, and kindly
offer your refuge
to an agitated heart. How well you reflect
the harshness of my fate in your lonely horror!
I see among the remnants
of shattered ships on this shore
an unknown warrior… I will listen to him,
comfort him, and
turn his grief into joy.

(He approaches and speaks to Idomeneo.)

Whoever you are, O warrior, cast aside your fear;
here ready to aid you is one
who in this land has the power to do so.

IDOMENEO *(aside)*

The more I look at him,
the more grief consumes me. *(to Idamante)* I will owe you
the rest of my life. And what reward
will you have from me?

83

IDAMANTE

Premio al mio cor sarà
l'esser pago d'averti
sollevato, difeso:
ahi troppo, amico,
dalle miserie mie instrutto io fui
a intenerirmi alle miserie altrui.

IDOMENEO *(da sé)*

Qual voce, qual pietà il mio sen trafigge!
(a Idamante) Misero tu? che dici? ti son conte
le tue sventure appien?

IDAMANTE

Dell'amor mio,
cielo! il più caro oggetto,
in quelli abissi spinto
giace l'eroe Idomeneo estinto.
Ma tu sospiri, e piangi?
T'è noto Idomeneo?

IDOMENEO

Uom più di questo
deplorabil non v'è, non v'è chi plachi
il fato suo austero.

IDAMANTE

Che favelli?
Vive egli ancor? *(da sé)* Oh Dei! torno a sperar.
Ah dimmi, amico, dimmi,
dov'è? dove quel dolce aspetto
vita mi renderà?

IDOMENEO

Ma donde nasce
questa che per lui nutri
tenerezza d'amor?

IDAMANTE

Potessi almeno
a lui stesso gl'affetti miei spiegare!

IDAMANTE

My heart's reward

will be to know that I
have comforted and defended you:
ah, my friend,
I have learnt from my own misfortunes
to be moved by those of others.

IDOMENEO *(aside)*

That voice, that compassion pierce me to the heart!
(to Idamante) You, unhappy? What are you saying?
Have you known so many misfortunes?

IDAMANTE

The dearest object

of my love, oh heavens,
thrust into those depths,
the hero Idomeneo, lies dead.
But you sigh, you weep?
Do you know Idomeneo?

IDOMENEO

No man is more

to be pitied than he, and none can mitigate
his stern fate.

IDAMANTE

What are you saying?

Is he still alive? *(aside)* Oh gods! I hope once more.
Ah, tell me, my friend, tell me,
where is he? Where is that sweet countenance
which will restore me to life?

IDOMENEO

But for what reason

do you bear him
such tender love?

IDAMANTE

If only I could

explain my affection to him!

IDOMENEO *(da sé)*
　　Pur quel sembiante
　　non m'è tutto stranier, un non so che
　　ravviso in quel…

IDAMANTE *(da sé)*
　　　　　　Pensoso il mesto sguardo
　　in me egli fissa… e pur a quella voce,
　　a quel ciglio, a quel gesto uom mi rassembra
　　o in corte, o altrove a me noto, ed amico.

IDOMENEO
　　Tu mediti.

IDAMANTE
　　　　　Tu mi contempli, e taci.

IDOMENEO
　　Perché quel tuo parlar sì mi conturba?

IDAMANTE
　　E qual mi sento anch'io
　　turbamento nell'alma? Ah più non posso
　　il pianto ritener. *(piange)*

IDOMENEO
　　　　　　Ma di': qual fonte
　　sgorga quel pianto? e quel sì acerbo duol,
　　che per Idomeneo tanto t'affligge…

IDAMANTE *(con enfasi)*
　　Ah, ch'egli è il padre…

IDOMENEO *(interrompendolo impaziente)*
　　　　　　Oh Dio!
　　Parla: di chi è egli il padre?

IDAMANTE *(con voce fiacca)*
　　　　　　È il padre mio!

IDOMENEO *(da sé)*
　　Spietatissimi Dei!

[0a]

IDOMENEO *(aside)*
 Yet those features
 are not entirely unknown to me; I recognize
 something in them…

IDAMANTE *(aside)*
 Pensively he fixes his sad gaze
 on me… and that voice,
 that look, that bearing remind me of someone
 I knew and loved, at court or elsewhere.

IDOMENEO
 You are lost in thought.

IDAMANTE

      You gaze at me and are silent.

IDOMENEO
 Why do your words so trouble me?

IDAMANTE
 And why do I too feel
 such trouble in my soul? Ah, I can no longer
 hold back my tears. *(he weeps)*

IDOMENEO

     But tell me: what is the source
 whence flow these tears? And the bitter grief
 which so afflicts you for Idomeneo…

IDAMANTE *(emphatically)*
 Ah, he is the father…

IDOMENEO *(interrupting him impatiently)*
      Oh God!
 Speak: whose father is he?

IDAMANTE *(in a weak voice)*
      He is my father!

IDOMENEO *(aside)*
 Most merciless gods!

IDAMANTE
                    Meco compiangi
    del padre mio il destin?

IDOMENEO *(dolente)*
    Ah figlio!…

IDAMANTE *(tutto giulivo)*
                    Ah padre!… ah Numi!
    Dove son io?… oh qual trasporto!… soffri,

(vuole abbracciarlo; il padre si ritira turbato)

    genitor adorato, che al tuo seno…
    e che un amplesso… ahimè! perché ti sdegni?
    Disperato mi fuggi?… ah dove, ah dove?

IDOMENEO
    Non mi seguir, te'l vieto:
    meglio per te saria il non avermi
    veduto or qui. Paventa il rivedermi!

(parte in fretta)

IDAMANTE
    Ah qual gelido orror m'ingombra i sensi!…
    Lo vedo appena, il riconosco, e a' miei
    teneri accenti in un balen s'invola.
    Misero! in che l'offesi, e come mai
    quel sdegno io meritai, quelle minacce?…
    Vuo' seguirlo e veder, oh sorte dura!
    Qual mi sovrasti ancor più rea sventura.

N°7 *Aria*

    Il padre adorato   [7]
        ritrovo, e lo perdo.
        Mi fugge sdegnato
        fremendo d'orror.
    Morire credei
        di gioia e d'amore;
        or, barbari Dei!
        m'uccide il dolor.

(parte addolorato)

IDAMANTE
                    Do you lament with me
    my father's fate?

IDOMENEO *(sorrowfully)*
    Ah, my son!

IDAMANTE *(full of joy)*
            Ah, my father! Ah, gods!
    Where am I? Oh, what rapture! Allow me,

(he seeks to embrace him; his father stands back, troubled)

    my adored father, on your bosom...
    an embrace... Alas, why do you disdain me?
    You run from me in despair? But where, oh where?

IDOMENEO
    Do not follow me, I forbid it:
    it would have been better for you
    not to have seen me here. Beware of seeing me again!

(exit in haste)

IDAMANTE
    Ah, what icy horror weighs on my senses!
    Hardly have I seen and recognized him than
    he flees my tender words in a flash.
    Woe is me! How have I offended him, and how
    have I deserved this anger, these threats?
    I will follow him and see, oh harsh fate,
    what still crueller misfortune awaits me.

No. 7 Aria

    My beloved father   [7]
        I find again, then I lose him.
        He angrily flees me,
        trembling with horror.
    I thought I would die
        of joy and love;
        now, cruel gods,
        sorrow is killing me.

(exit sorrowfully)

INTERMEZZO

Il mare è tutto tranquillo. Sbarcano le truppe cretesi arrivate con Idomeneo. I guerrieri cantano il seguente coro in onore di Nettuno. Le donne cretesi accorrono ad abbracciare i loro felicemente arrivati, e sfogano la vicendevole gioia con un ballo generale, che termina col coro. Marcia guerriera durante lo sbarco. Coro de' guerrieri sbarcati

N°8 *Marcia* [8]

N°9 *Coro*

TUTTI

   Nettuno s'onori, [9]
      quel nome risuoni,
      quel nume s'adori,
      sovrano del mar.
      Con danze e con suoni
      convien festeggiar.

SOLI

   Da lunge ei mira
      di Giove l'ira,
      e in un baleno
      va all'Eghe in seno,
      da regal sede
      tosto provvede,
      fa i generosi
      destrier squamosi
      ratto accoppiar.
   Dall'onde fuore
      suonan sonore
      tritoni araldi
      robusti e baldi
      buccine intorno.
      Già ride il giorno
      che il gran tridente
      il mar furente
      seppe domar.

INTERMEZZO

The sea is quite calm. The Cretan troops who arrived with Idomeneo disembark. The warriors sing the following chorus in honour of Neptune. The Cretan women run to embrace their menfolk happily restored to them, and express their joy at seeing one another in a general dance, which is concluded by the chorus. Warlike march during the landing. Chorus of disembarked warriors

No. 8 March [8]

No. 9 Chorus

ALL

    Let Neptune be honoured! [9]
      Let his name resound,
      and let that god,
      monarch of the sea, be adored.
      With dances and music
      it is right to celebrate him.

SOLOISTS

    From afar he observes
      Jove's anger,
      and in a flash
      descends to the bosom of the Aegean;
      from his royal throne
      he soon makes all ready,
      and has his noble,
      scaly steeds
      swiftly yoked.
    From out of the waves,
      herald Tritons,
      sturdy and bold,
      blow their trumpets
      which resound all around.
      Already day returns,
      for the great trident
      has subdued
      the raging sea.

TUTTI

Nettuno s'onori,
    quel nome risuoni,
    quel nume s'adori,
    sovrano del mar.
    Con danze e con suoni
    convien festeggiar.

SOLI

Su conca d'oro,
    regio decoro
    spira Nettuno.
    Scherza Portuno
    ancor bambino
    col suo delfino,
    con Anfitrite.
    Or noi di Dite
    fé trionfar.
Nereidi amabili,
    ninfe adorabili,
    che alla gran Dea
    con Galatea
    corteggio fate,
    deh ringraziate
    per noi quei Numi,
    che i nostri lumi
    fero asciugar.

TUTTI

Nettuno s'onori,
    quel nome risuoni,
    quel nume s'adori,
    sovrano del mar.
    Con danze e con suoni
    convien festeggiar.
Or suonin le trombe,
    solenne ecatombe
    andiam preparar.

ALL

    Let Neptune be honoured!
      Let his name resound,
      and let that god,
      monarch of the sea, be adored.
      With dances and music
      it is right to celebrate him.

SOLOISTS

    On a golden conch,
      his royal emblem,
      Neptune blows.
      Portunus,*
      still a child,
      plays with his dolphin
      along with Amphitrite.*
      Now he has made us
      victorious over Dis.*
    Lovely Nereids,
      adorable nymphs,
      who with Galatea
      make up the train
      of the great goddess,
      pray give thanks
      for us to these gods
      who have allowed us
      to dry the tears from our eyes.

ALL

    Let Neptune be honoured!
      Let his name resound,
      and let that god,
      monarch of the sea, be adored.
      With dances and music
      it is right to celebrate him.
    Now let the trumpets sound,
      let us go to prepare
      solemn sacrifices.

ATTO SECONDO

[Munich version, 1781]

Scena I

Appartamenti reali.
Idomeneo, Arbace

IDOMENEO
>Siam soli. Odimi, Arbace, e il grand'arcano
>in sen racchiudi; assai
>per lungo uso m'è nota
>tua fedeltà.

ARBACE
>   Di fedeltà il vassallo
>merto non ha: virtù non è il dover.
>Ecco la vita, il sangue...

IDOMENEO
>Un sol consiglio or mi fa d'uopo. Ascolta:
>tu sai quanto a' Troiani
>fu il brando mio fatal.

ARBACE
>   Tutto m'è noto.

IDOMENEO
>Gonfio di tante imprese
>al varco alfin m'attese il fier Nettuno...

ARBACE
>E so che a' danni tuoi,
>ad Eolo unito e a Giove,
>il suo regno sconvolse...

ACT TWO

Scene I

The royal apartments.
Idomeneo, Arbace

IDOMENEO

We are alone. Listen to me, Arbace,
and enfold this great secret in your bosom;
I have long known
your fidelity.

ARBACE

Fidelity in a subject
has no merit: duty is not a virtue.
Here is my life, my blood...

IDOMENEO

For the moment I need only advice.
Listen: you know how fatal
my sword was to the Trojans.

ARBACE

I know very well.

IDOMENEO

I was puffed up with pride at such feats,
but in the end fierce Neptune lay in wait for me.

ARBACE

And I know that, to your undoing,
allying himself with Aeolus and Jupiter,
he threw his kingdom into turmoil...

IDOMENEO
Sì, che m'estorse in voto
umana vittima.

ARBACE
Di chi?

IDOMENEO
Del primo,
che sulla spiaggia incauto a me s'appressi.

ARBACE
Or dimmi:
chi primo tu incontrasti?

IDOMENEO
Inorridisci:
il mio figlio…

ARBACE *(perdendosi d'animo)*
Idamante!… Io vengo meno…

(raccoltosi)

Ti vide? Il conoscesti?

IDOMENEO
Mi vide, e a offrirmi ogni sollievo accorse,
credendomi stranier, e il morto padre
piangendo, al lungo ragionar l'un l'altro
conobbe alfin, ahi conoscenza…

ARBACE
A lui
il suo destin svelasti?

IDOMENEO
No, che da orror confuso io m'involai,
disperato il lasciai.

ARBACE
Povero padre!
Idamante infelice!

IDOMENEO
> Yes, and he extorted from me, as a tribute,
> a human sacrifice.

ARBACE
> Of whom?

IDOMENEO
> Of the first person
> who should rashly approach me on the shore.

ARBACE
> Now tell me:
> whom did you meet first?

IDOMENEO
> You will be struck with horror:
> my son...

ARBACE *(overcome)*
> Idamante!... I grow faint...

(collecting himself)

> Did he see you? Did he recognize you?

IDOMENEO
> He saw me, and hastened to offer me comfort,
> believing me to be a stranger, and weeping
> for his dead father. Eventually, as we spoke, we recognized
> one another; alas, terrible recognition...

ARBACE
> Did you
> reveal his fate to him?

IDOMENEO
> No, for I fled, overwhelmed by horror,
> and left him in despair.

ARBACE
> Poor father!
> Unhappy Idamante!

IDOMENEO
Dammi Arbace il consiglio,
salvami, per pietà, salvami il figlio.

ARBACE *(pensa, poi risolve)*
Trovisi in altro clima altro soggiorno.

IDOMENEO
Dura necessità!… Ma dove mai,
dove ad occhio immortal potrà celarsi?

ARBACE
Purché al popol si celi.
Per altra via intanto
Nettun si placherà, qualche altro nume
di lui cura n'avrà.

IDOMENEO
                    Ben dici, è vero…

(Vede venire Ilia.)

Ilia s'apressa, ahimè!…

(Resta un poco pensoso e poi decide.)

In Argo ei vada, e sul paterno soglio
rimetta Elettra… Or vanne a lei e al figlio,
fa' che sian pronti. Il tutto
sollecito disponi.
Custodisci l'arcano. A te mi fido.
A te dovranno, oh caro, oh fido Arbace,
la vita il figlio, e il genitor la pace.

N°10a Aria

ARBACE
Se il tuo duol, se il mio desìo   [10a]
    sen volassero del pari,
    a ubbidirti qual son io,
    saria il duol pronto a fuggir.
Quali al trono sian compagni
    chi l'ambisce or veda e impari:
    stia lontan, o non si lagni,
    se non trova che martir. *(parte)*

IDOMENEO
> Give me your counsel, Arbace;
> save me, for pity's sake, save my son.

ARBACE *(thinks, then decides)*
> Let him find another home, in another country.

IDOMENEO
> Harsh necessity! But where on earth,
> where can he hide from immortal eyes?

ARBACE
> As long as he is hidden from the people,
> in the meantime, Neptune will be appeased
> in some other way, and some other god
> will protect him.

IDOMENEO
> You speak well, it is true...

(He sees Ilia approaching.)

> Ilia is coming, alas!

(He remains thoughtful a while, then is resolved.)

> Let him go to Argos and restore Elettra
> to her father's throne... Go to her and my son,
> let them make ready. Let all
> be arranged rapidly.
> Keep this secret. I place my trust in you.
> To you, dear, faithful Arbace, the son will owe
> his life, and the father his peace of mind.

No. 10a Aria

ARBACE
> If your grief and my zeal   [10a]
>> went hand in hand,
>> your grief would be as eager to vanish
>> as I am to obey you.
> Let whoever aspires to the throne
>> see and learn what accompanies it:
>> let him keep his distance, or not complain
>> if he finds only suffering there. *(exit)*

[Vienna version, 1786]

Scena I

Ilia, Idamante

N°10b Scena con Rondò (K490)

ILIA

> Non più. Tutto ascoltai, tutto compresi.
> D'Elettra e d'Idamante
> noti sono gli amori,
> al caro impegno omai mancar non dêi,
> va', scordati di me, dónati a lei.

IDAMANTE

> Ch'io mi scordi di te? Che a lei mi doni
> puoi consigliarmi? e puoi voler ch'io viva?

ILIA

> Non congiurar, mia vita,
> contro la mia costanza. Il colpo atroce
> mi distrugge abbastanza.

IDAMANTE

>   Ah no, sarebbe
> il viver mio di morte assai peggior.
> Fosti il mio primo amore,
> e l'ultimo sarai. Venga la morte,
> intrepido l'attendo,
> ma, ch'io possa struggermi ad altra face,
> ad altr'oggetto donar gl'affetti miei,
> come tentarlo? Ah, di dolor morrei.

Rondò

IDAMANTE

> Non temer, amato bene,   [10b]
> > per te sempre il cor sarà.
> > Più non reggo a tante pene,
> > l'alma mia mancando va.

[Vienna version, 1786]

Scene I

Ilia, Idamante

No. 10b Scena with rondò (K490)

ILIA

No more. I have heard all, have understood all.
The love of Elettra and Idamante
is well known.
You may no longer neglect your cherished pledge;
go, forget me, give yourself to her.

IDAMANTE

Should I forget you? Can you counsel me
to give myself to her, and then wish me to live on?

ILIA

My life, do not try
my steadfastness. The dreadful blow
already afflicts me enough.

IDAMANTE

Ah no, it would be
far worse than death for me to live on.
You were my first love,
and you will be my last. Let death come,
I await it fearlessly;
but that I could be consumed by another flame,
could give my love to another –
how could you suggest that? Ah, I would die of grief.

Rondò

IDAMANTE

Fear not, my beloved,   [10b]
my heart will always be yours.
I can no longer bear such suffering;
my spirit grows faint.

Tu sospiri? oh duol funesto!
Pensa almen che istante è questo!
Non mi posso, oh Dio, spiegar.

Non temer, amato bene,
per te sempre il cor sarà.
Stelle barbare, spietate,
perchè mai tanto rigor?

Alme belle che vedete
le mie pene in tal momento,
dite voi, s'egual tormento
può soffrir un fido cor. *(parte)*

Scena II

Idomeneo, Ilia

ILIA

Se mai pomposo apparse
su l'argivo orizzonte il Dio di Delo,
eccolo in questo giorno, oh sire, in cui
l'augusta tua presenza i tuoi diletti
sudditi torna in vita e lor pupille,
che ti piansero estinto, or rasserena.

IDOMENEO

Principessa gentil, il bel sereno
anche alle tue pupille omai ritorni.
Il lungo duol dilegua.

ILIA

                    Io piansi, è vero,
e invano l'are tue,
oh glauca Dea, bagnai:
Ecuba genitrice, ah tu lo sai!
Piansi in veder l'antico
Priamo genitor dell'armi sotto
al grave incarco, al suo partir, al tristo
avviso di sua morte, e piansi poi
al vedere nel tempio il ferro, il fuoco,

You sigh? Oh bitter grief!
   Think at least what this moment means!
   Oh heavens, I cannot explain.

Fear not, my beloved,
   my heart will always be yours.
   Cruel, pitiless stars,
   why are you so severe?

Kind souls who see
   my sufferings at this moment,
   say whether a faithful heart
   can endure such torment. *(exit)*

Scene II

Idomeneo, Ilia

ILIA
   If ever the god of Delos* appeared in splendour
   on the Greek horizon,
   it is today, sire, when
   your august presence restores
   your dear subjects to life, and you brighten
   their eyes which mourned you as dead.

IDOMENEO
   Noble princess, may serenity
   now return to your eyes too.
   Make an end of your long suffering.

ILIA
                        I have wept, it is true,
   and it is in vain that I bathed
   your altars with my tears, O grey-eyed goddess:*
   Hecuba, my mother, well you know it!
   I wept to see my old father
   Priam beneath so heavy a burden
   of arms, at his parting,
   at the sad news of his death; and then I wept
   to see fire and sword in the temple,

la patria distrutta, e me rapita
in questa acerba età,
fra nemici e tempeste, prigioniera
sotto un polo stranier...

IDOMENEO

                    Assai soffristi...
Ma ogni trista memoria or si sbandisca.

ILIA

Poiché il tuo amabil figlio
libertà mi donò, di grazie e onori
mi ricolmò, tutta de' tuoi la gioia
in me raccolta io sento. Eccomi, accetta
l'omaggio, ed in tributo
il mio, non più infelice,
ma avventurato cor
al figlio, al genitor grato e divoto.
Signor, se umile è il don, sincero è il voto.

IDOMENEO

Idamante mio figlio,
allor che libertà ti diè, non fu
che interprete felice
del paterno voler. S'ei mi prevenne,
quanto ei fece a tuo pro tutto io confermo.
Di me, de' miei tesori,
Ilia, disponi, e mia cura sarà,
dartene chiare prove
dell'amicizia mia.

ILIA

Son certa, e un dubbio in me colpa saria.
Propizie stelle! Qual benigno influsso
la sorte mia cangiò? Dove temei
strazio e morte incontrar, lieta rinasco,
colgo, dove credei avverso il tutto,
delle amare mie pene il dolce frutto.

my homeland destroyed, and myself
abducted so young,
amid enemies and storms, a prisoner
under foreign skies...

IDOMENEO

You have suffered much...
But let all sad memories be banished now.

ILIA

Since your amiable son
has given me my freedom and heaped
favours and honours on me, I feel within me
all the joy of your people. Behold me: accept
my homage, and in tribute
my heart, no longer unhappy,
but fortunate,
grateful and devoted to both son and father.
Lord, though the gift be humble, the vow is sincere.

IDOMENEO

My son Idamante,
when he gave you your freedom, was merely
the felicitous interpreter
of his father's will. If he anticipated me,
I fully confirm all he did for you.
Myself and all my treasures,
Ilia, are at your disposal, and it will be my care
to offer you certain proof
of my friendship.

ILIA

I am sure of that, and would be wrong to doubt it.
Propitious stars! What benign influence
has changed my destiny? Where I feared
to meet torment and death, I am reborn joyful,
and, where I thought all was against me, I pluck
the sweet fruit of my bitter sufferings.

N°11 Aria

    Se il padre perdei,   [11a]
       la patria, il riposo,
       tu padre mi sei,

(ad Idomeneo)

    soggiorno amoroso   [11b]
    è Creta per me.
    Or più non rammento
    le angosce, gl'affanni.
    Or gioia e contento,
    compenso a' miei danni
    il cielo mi diè. *(parte)*

Scena III

Idomeneo solo

IDOMENEO

    Qual mi conturba i sensi   [12a]
    equivoca favella?… Ne' suoi casi
    qual mostra a un tratto intempestiva gioa
    la frigia principessa?… E quei ch'esprime
    teneri sentimenti per il prence,
    sarebber forse… ahimè…
    sentimenti d'amor, gioia di speme?…
    Non m'inganno. Reciproco è l'amore.
    Troppo, Idamante, a scior quelle catene
    sollecito tu fosti… ecco il delitto
    che in te punisce il ciel… Sì sì, a Nettuno
    il figlio, il padre ed Ilia
    tre vittime saran su l'ara istessa
    da egual dolor afflitte,
    una dal ferro, e due dal duol trafitte.

N°12 Aria

    Fuor del mar ho un mar in seno,   [12b]
       che del primo è più funesto.
       E Nettuno ancora in questo
       mai non cessa minacciar.

No. 11 Aria

> Though I have lost my father,   [11a, 11b]
> > my homeland, my tranquillity,
> > you are a father to me,

(to Idomeneo)

> > and Crete is for me
> > a haven of affection.
> Now I no longer recall
> > my anguish, my trouble.
> > Now Heaven gives me
> > joy and contentment
> > to compensate my loss. *(exit)*

Scene III

Idomeneo alone

IDOMENEO

> Why do these ambiguous words   [12a]
> trouble my mind?... Why, in her situation,
> does the Phrygian princess suddenly show
> such untimely joy?... And these tender feelings
> she expresses for the prince,
> could they perhaps be, alas,
> feelings of love, the joy born of hope?...
> I am not mistaken. Their love is mutual.
> You were too quick, Idamante, to break
> those chains... That is the crime
> that Heaven punishes in you... Yes, yes, on the same altar,
> the son, the father and Ilia
> will all three be victims to Neptune,
> afflicted with the same sorrow:
> one pierced by the sword, and two by grief.

No. 12 Aria

> Though saved from the sea, I have a sea in my breast   [12b]
> > that is more terrible than the first.
> > And in that sea too, Neptune
> > never ceases to threaten me.

Fiero nume! dimmi almeno:
se al naufragio è sì vicino
il mio cor, qual rio destino
or gli vieta il naufragar?

Frettolosa e giuliva
Elettra vien. S'ascolti.

Scena IV

Idomeneo, Elettra

ELETTRA
Sire, da Arbace intesi
quanto la tua clemenza
s'interessa per me. Già all'infinito
giunser le grazie tue, l'obbligo mio.
Or, tua mercé, verdeggia in me la speme
di vedere ben tosto
depresso de' ribelli il folle orgoglio.
E come a tanto amore
corrisponder potrò?

IDOMENEO
                    Di tua difesa
ha l'impegno Idamante, a lui men vado,
farò che adempia or or l'intento mio,
il suo dover, e appaghi il tuo disio. *(parte)*

Scena V

Elettra sola

ELETTRA
Chi mai del mio provò piacer più dolce?
Parto, e l'unico oggetto
che amo ed adoro, oh Dei!
meco sen vien? Ah, troppo
troppo angusto è il mio cor a tanta gioia!
Lunge dalla rivale
farò ben io, con vezzi e con lusinghe,
che quel fuoco che pria

Fierce god! Tell me at least:
  if my heart is so close
  to shipwreck, what evil destiny
  now prevents it from foundering?

Here comes Elettra in haste
and joy. Let me listen to her.

Scene IV

Idomeneo, Elettra

ELETTRA
  Sire, I have learnt from Arbace
  how great is your kindness
  towards me. Your benefits to me
  and my obligations to you are already infinite.
  Now, thanks to you, hope revives within me
  that I will soon see
  the mad ambition of the rebels crushed.
  How can I reciprocate
  such loving kindness?

IDOMENEO
                    The task of defending you
  is entrusted to Idamante; I go to him,
  and will ensure that he carries out my intentions
  and his duty, and gratifies your wishes. *(exit)*

Scene V

Elettra alone

ELETTRA
  Who ever felt sweeter pleasure than mine?
  I am leaving, and the sole object
  of my love and adoration, oh gods,
  is coming with me? Ah, my heart
  is too small to contain such joy!
  Far from my rival,
  I will succeed, with charms and endearments,
  in making that flame

spegnere non potei,
a quei lumi s'estingua, e avvampi ai miei.

N°13 Aria

Idol mio! se ritroso   [13]
    altra amante a me ti rende,
    non m'offende rigoroso,
    più m'alletta austero amor.
Scaccerà vicino ardore
    dal tuo sen l'ardor lontano;
    più la mano può d'Amore
    s'è vicin l'amante cor.

No. 14. Marcia

(S'ode da lontano armoniosa marcia.)   [14]

ELETTRA
    Odo da lunge armonioso suono
    che mi chiama all'imbarco. Orsù, si vada.

*(Parte in fretta. Si sente sempre più vicina la marcia a misura che si
muta la scena.)*

Scena VI

Porto di Sidone con bastimenti lungo le spiagge.
Elettra, truppa d'Argivi, di Cretesi e de' marinari.

ELETTRA
    Sidonie sponde! O voi,
    per me di pianto e duol, d'amor nemico
    crudo ricetto, or che astro più clemente
    a voi mi toglie, io vi perdono e in pace
    al lieto partir mio
    alfin vi lascio e do l'estremo addio!

N°15 Coro

TUTTI
    Placido è il mar, andiamo;   [15]
        tutto ci rassicura.
        Felice avrem ventura,
        sù sù, partiamo or or.

which I could not extinguish until now
die out for her eyes, and rekindle it for mine.

No. 13 Aria

My idol, if your other lover   [13]
  yields you to me as a reluctant suitor,
  such rigour does not deter me;
  a stern love attracts me more.
Passion close to you will chase
  the more distant passion from your heart;
  the hand of Love has greater power
  if the heart that loves is near.

No. 14 March

(A melodious march is heard in the distance.)   [14]

ELETTRA
  I hear from afar sweet music
  that summons me aboard ship. Let me go, then.

*(Exit in haste. The march is heard ever closer as the scene
changes.)*

Scene VI

The port of Cydonia, with ships along the shoreline.
Elettra, a crowd of Greeks, Cretans and sailors

ELETTRA
  Shores of Cydonia! You who were
  but a harsh refuge for my tears and sorrows,
  my frustrated love, now that a kinder star
  takes me from you, I forgive you, and in peace,
  on my joyful departure,
  at last I leave you and bid you a final farewell!

No. 15 Chorus

ALL
  The sea is calm, let us depart;   [15]
    everything reassures us.
    We will have good fortune;
    come, come, let us leave at once.

ELETTRA
    Soavi Zeffiri
      soli spirate,
      del freddo Borea
      l'ira calmate.
      D'aura piacevole
      cortesi siate,
      se da voi spargesi
      per tutto amor.

TUTTI
    Placido è il mar, andiamo;
      tutto ci rassicura.
      Felice avrem ventura,
      sù sù, partiamo or or.

Scena VII

Idomeneo, Idamante, Elettra. Seguito del re

IDOMENEO
    Vattene prence.

IDAMANTE
              Oh ciel!

IDOMENEO
                    Troppo t'arresti.
    Parti, e non dubbia fama
    di mille eroiche imprese il tuo ritorno
    prevenga. Di regnare
    se l'arte apprender vuoi, ora incomincia
    a renderti de' miseri il sostegno,
    del padre e di te stesso ognor più degno.

N°16 Terzetto

IDAMANTE
    Pria di partir, oh Dio!   [16]
      soffri che un bacio imprima
      su la paterna man.

ELETTRA
    Gentle Zephyrs,
        you alone must blow
        and calm the anger
        of chilly Boreas;*
        with your pleasant breath
        be kind to us;
        through your agency
        let love spread everywhere.

ALL
    The sea is calm, let us depart;
        everything reassures us.
        We will have good fortune;
        come, come, let us leave at once.

Scene VII

Idomeneo, Idamante, Elettra. The king's retinue.

IDOMENEO
    Go now, prince.

IDAMANTE
                Oh Heaven!

IDOMENEO
                        You delay too long.
    Go, and let the undoubted renown
    of a thousand heroic deeds herald
    your return. If you would learn
    the art of ruling, begin now
    by making yourself the support of the unfortunate,
    ever worthier of your father and yourself.

No. 16 Trio

IDAMANTE
    Before I leave – oh God! –   [16]
        allow me to place a kiss
        on my father's hand.

113

ELETTRA
Soffri che un grato addio
sul labbro il cor esprima:
addio, degno sovran!

IDOMENEO *(ad Elettra)*
Vanne, sarai felice,
Figlio! tua sorte è questa.

IDAMANTE, ELETTRA, IDOMENEO *(a tre)*
Seconda i voti, oh ciel!

ELETTRA
Quanto sperar mi lice!

IDAMANTE
Vado! *(da sé)* e il mio cor qui resta.

IDAMANTE, ELETTRA, IDOMENEO *(a tre)*
Addio!

IDOMENEO, IDAMANTE *(a due)*
(ognuno da sé)
Destin crudel!

IDAMANTE *(da sé)*
Oh Ilia!

IDOMENEO *(da sé)*
Oh figlio!

IDAMANTE
Oh padre! oh partenza!

ELETTRA
Oh Dei! che sarà?

TUTTI
Deh cessi il scompiglio;
del ciel la clemenza
sua man porgerà.

(Vanno verso le navi. Mentre vanno ad imbarcarsi sorge improvvisa tempesta. Il popolo canta il seguente.)

ELETTRA
Allow my heart to express through my lips
a grateful farewell:
farewell, noble sovereign!

IDOMENEO *(to Elettra)*
Go, you will be happy.
My son! This is your destiny.

IDAMANTE, ELETTRA, IDOMENEO *(together)*
Grant our prayers, O Heaven!

ELETTRA
What great hopes are mine!

IDAMANTE
I go! *(aside)* But my heart remains here.

IDAMANTE, ELETTRA, IDOMENEO *(together)*
Farewell!

IDAMANTE, IDOMENEO *(together)*
(aside)
Cruel fate!

IDAMANTE *(aside)*
Oh, Ilia!

IDOMENEO *(aside)*
Oh, my son!

IDAMANTE
Oh, my father! Oh parting!

ELETTRA
Oh gods! What will befall us?

ALL
Come, let this agitation cease:
from Heaven above, clemency
will extend its hand to us.

(They go towards the ships. As they are about to embark, a sudden storm arises. The people sing the following chorus.)

115

N°17 Coro

CORO

Qual nuovo terrore!
qual rauco muggito!
De' Numi il furore
ha il mare infierito.
Nettuno, mercé!

(Incalza la tempesta, il mare si gonfia, il cielo tuona e lampeggia, e i frequenti fulmini incendiano le navi. Un mostro formidabile s'appresenta fuori dell'onde. Il popolo canta il seguente.)

Qual odio, qual ira
Nettuno ci mostra!
Se il cielo s'adira,
qual colpa è la nostra?
Il reo, qual è? [17]

IDOMENEO

Eccoti in me, barbaro nume! il reo.
Io solo errai, me sol punisci e cada
sopra di me il tuo sdegno. La mia morte
ti sazi alfin; ma s'altra aver pretendi
vittima al fallo mio, una innocente
darti io non posso e, se pur tu la vuoi,
ingiusto sei, pretenderla non puoi.

(La tempesta continua. I Cretesi spaventati fuggono, e nel seguente coro col canto e con pantomime esprimono il loro terrore, ciò che tutto forma un'azione analoga e chiude l'atto col solito divertimento.)

N°18 Coro

CORO

Corriamo, fuggiamo [18, 0c]
quel mostro spietato.
Corriamo, fuggiamo,
Ah preda già siamo!
Chi, perfido fato!
più crudo è di te?

No. 17 Chorus

CHORUS
    What new terror!
      What hoarse roaring!
      The fury of the gods
      has whipped up the sea.
      Neptune, have mercy!

(The storm mounts, the sea swells, there is thunder and lightning. The frequent thunderbolts set the ships on fire. A fearsome monster emerges from the waves. The people sing the following chorus.)

    What hate, what anger
      Neptune shows us!
      If Heaven rages so,
      what sin have we committed?
      Who is the guilty one?   [17]

IDOMENEO
    Behold in me, cruel god, the guilty one!
    I alone have sinned: punish me alone; let your wrath
    fall on me. May my death
    satisfy you at last; but if you claim another victim
    for my fault, I cannot give you
    an innocent; and if you still wish him,
    you are unjust, and cannot claim him.

(The storm continues. The frightened Cretans flee, and, in the following chorus, they express their terror in song and mime, so that the whole forms an appropriate end to the act, closing it with the customary divertissement.)

No. 18 Chorus

CHORUS
    Let us run, let us flee   [18, 0c]
      that pitiless monster.
    Let us run, let us flee:
      ah, we are already its prey!
      Treacherous fate,
      who is crueller than you?

ATTO TERZO

Scena I

Giardino reale.
Ilia sola

ILIA

Solitudini amiche, aure amorose,
piante fiorite e fiori vaghi, udite
d'una infelice amante
i lamenti che a voi lassa confido.
Quanto il tacer presso al mio vincitore,
quanto il finger ti costa, afflitto core!

N°19 Aria

Zeffiretti lusinghieri,   [19]
    deh volate al mio tesoro
    e gli dite ch'io l'adoro,
    che mi serbi il cor fedel.
E voi piante e fior sinceri,
    che ora innaffia il pianto amaro,
    dite a lui che amor più raro
    mai vedeste sotto al ciel.

Ei stesso vien... oh Dei... Mi spiego o taccio?
Resto?... parto?... o m'ascondo?...
Ah risolver non posso, ah mi confondo!

Scena II

Ilia, Idamante

IDAMANTE

Principessa, a' tuoi sguardi
se offrirmi ardisco ancor, più non mi guida

118

ACT THREE

Scene I

The royal garden.
Ilia alone

ILIA

Friendly solitude, loving breezes,
blossoming trees and pretty flowers, hear
the laments of an unhappy lover
which, alas, I confide to you.
How much it costs my afflicted heart
to be silent and dissemble when near my conqueror!

No. 19 Aria

Flattering zephyrs,   [19]
   ah, fly to my treasure
   and tell him I adore him,
   and to keep his heart true to me.
And you, trees and honest flowers
   which my bitter tears now water,
   tell him that you never saw
   a rarer love beneath the sky.

He is coming! Oh gods! Must I speak or be silent?
Should I stay? Or leave? Or conceal myself?...
Ah, I cannot decide, I am confused!

Scene II

Ilia, Idamante

IDAMANTE

Princess, if I dare to offer myself to your sight
once more, I am no longer guided

119

un temerario affetto. Altro or non cerco
che appagarti e morir.

ILIA

Morir? tu, prence?

IDAMANTE

Più teco io resto, più di te m'accendo,
e s'aggrava mia colpa; a che il castigo
più a lungo differir?

ILIA

Ma qual cagione
morte a cercar t'induce?

IDAMANTE

Il genitore
pien di smania e furore
torvo mi guarda e fugge,
e il motivo mi cela.
Da tue catene avvinto, il tuo rigore
a nuovi guai m'espone. Un fiero mostro
fa dappertutto orrida strage. Or questo
a combatter si vada
e vincerlo si tenti,
o finisca la morte i miei tormenti.

ILIA

Calma, oh prence, un trasporto sì funesto:
rammenta che tu sei d'un grand'impero
l'unica speme.

IDAMANTE

Privo del tuo amore,
privo, Ilia, di te, nulla mi cale.

ILIA

Misera me!... deh serba i giorni tuoi.

IDAMANTE

Il mio fato crudel seguir degg'io.

by rash emotion. I now seek nothing else
than to placate you, and die.

ILIA

Die? You, prince?

IDAMANTE

The more I stay with you, the more I burn for you,
and the greater my guilt becomes; why defer
punishment any longer?

ILIA

But what is it
that prompts you to seek death?

IDAMANTE

My father,
full of agitation and fury,
looks at me grimly and avoids me
without telling me why.
Since my heart is your captive, your severity
causes me new woes. A dreadful monster
commits horrible carnage far and wide. Now I go
to fight it
and try to overcome it,
or else death will put an end to my torments.

ILIA

O prince, calm this transport of grief:
remember that you are the sole hope
of a great empire.

IDAMANTE

Deprived of your love,
deprived of you, Ilia, nothing matters to me.

ILIA

Woe is me! I pray you, preserve your life.

IDAMANTE

I must follow my cruel destiny.

ILIA

    Vivi… Ilia te'l chiede.

IDAMANTE

                    Oh Dei! che ascolto?
    Principessa adorata!…

ILIA

                 Il cor turbato
    a te mal custodì
    la debolezza mia;
    purtroppo amore e tema
    indivisi ho nel sen.

IDAMANTE

    Odo? o sol quel che brama
    finge l'udito, o pure il grand'ardore
    m'agita i sensi, e il cor lusinga oppresso
    un dolce sogno?

ILIA

              Ah! perché pria non arsi
    che scoprir la mia fiamma? Mille io sento
    rimorsi all'alma. Il sacro mio dovere,
    la mia gloria, la patria, il sangue
    de' miei ancor fumante, oh quanto al core
    rimproverano il mio ribelle amore!…
    Ma al fin che fo? Già che in periglio estremo
    ti vedo, oh caro, e trarti sola io posso,
    odimi, io tel ridico:
    t'amo, t'adoro, e se morir tu vuoi,
    pria che m'uccida il duol morir non puoi.

              [Munich version, 1781]

N°20a *Duetto*

IDAMANTE

    S'io non moro a questi accenti,   [20a]
      non è ver, che amor uccida,
      che la gioia opprima un cor.

ILIA

    Live: Ilia asks it of you.

IDAMANTE

                  Oh gods! What do I hear?

    My beloved princess!

ILIA

                My troubled heart

    could not conceal from you

    my weakness;

    alas, love and fear

    are commingled in my bosom.

IDAMANTE

    Do I hear aright? Or do my ears merely think

    they heard what I desire? Or does ardent passion

    upset my senses, so that a sweet dream flatters

    my oppressed heart?

ILIA

              Ah, why did I not let myself be consumed

    rather than reveal my flame? I feel

    a thousand pangs of remorse. My sacred duty,

    my honour, my homeland, the still warm blood

    of my kinsfolk, oh, how they reproach

    my heart for its rebellious love!

    But what can I do? Since I see you, my dearest,

    in great danger, from which I alone can save you,

    listen to me, I tell you once more:

    I love you, I adore you, and if you wish to die,

    you will be unable to before grief kills me too.

[Munich version, 1781]

No. 20a Duet

IDAMANTE

    If I do not die at these words,   [20a]

      it is not true that love can kill

      and that joy can overwhelm the heart.

123

ILIA
> Non più duol, non più lamenti;
> io ti son costante e fida,
> tu sei il solo mio tesor.

IDAMANTE
> Tu sarai...

ILIA
> Qual tu mi vuoi.

IDAMANTE
> La mia sposa...

ILIA
> Lo sposo mio
sarai tu.

IDAMANTE, ILIA *(a due)*
> Lo dica amor.
Ah! il gioir sorpassa in noi
> il sofferto affanno rio,
> tutto vince il nostro ardor!

[Vienna version, 1786]

N°20b Duetto (K489)

ILIA
> Spiegarti non poss'io
> quanto il mio cor t'adora;
> ma il cor tacendo ancora
> potrà spiegarlo appien.

[20b]

IDAMANTE
> Voci dell'idol mio
> ah che in udirvi io sento
> d'insolito contento
> tutto inondarmi il sen.

ILIA
> Vita dell'alma mia...

ILIA

    No more sorrow, no more lamenting;
      I am constant and true to you,
      you are my only treasure.

IDAMANTE

    You will be...

ILIA

                  Whatever you want.

IDAMANTE

    My wife...

ILIA

              ...my husband
    you will be

IDAMANTE, ILIA *(together)*

          Let love proclaim it.
    Ah, our happiness overcomes
      the cruel affliction we have suffered.
      Our passion conquers all!

[Vienna version, 1786]

No. 20b Duet (K489)

ILIA

    I cannot tell you   [20b]
      how much my heart adores you;
      but that heart, even silent,
      will be able to tell you all.

IDAMANTE

    Words of my idol,
      ah, when I hear you, I feel
      unwonted happiness
      flooding my whole breast.

ILIA

    Life of my soul...

IDAMANTE
Delizia del mio cor,

ILIA, IDAMANTE *(a due)*
Non sa piacer che sia,
non sa che sia diletto,
chi non provò nel petto
sì fortunato amor.

Scena III

Idomeneo, Elettra, e detti

IDOMENEO *(da sé)*
Cieli! Che vedo!

ILIA *(a Idamante)*
Ah siam scoperti, oh caro.

IDAMANTE *(a Ilia)*
Non temer, idol mio.

ELETTRA *(da sé)*
Ecco l'ingrato.

IDOMENEO *(da sé)*
Io ben m'apposi al ver. Ah crudo fato!

IDAMANTE
Signor, già più non oso
padre chiamarti, a un suddito infelice
deh questa almen concedi
unica grazia.

IDOMENEO
Parla.

ELETTRA *(da sé)*
Che dirà?

IDAMANTE
In che t'offesi mai? Perché mi fuggi,
m'odi e aborrisci?

IDAMANTE
  Delight of my heart,

ILIA, IDAMANTE *(together)*
  He does not know what pleasure is,
    does not know what delight is,
    who has never felt in his bosom
    so happy a love as this.

Scene III

Idomeneo, Elettra, the previous

IDOMENEO *(aside)*
  Heavens! What do I see?

ILIA *(to Idamante)*
                    Ah, we are discovered, my dearest.

IDAMANTE *(to Ilia)*
  Have no fear, my idol.

ELETTRA *(aside)*
                    Behold the ingrate.

IDOMENEO *(aside)*
  So I was right. Ah, cruel fate!

IDAMANTE
  My lord, for I no longer dare
  call you father, at least grant
  an unhappy subject
  a single grace.

IDOMENEO
              Speak.

ELETTRA *(aside)*
                What will he say?

IDAMANTE
  How have I offended you? Why do you shun me,
  hate and abhor me?

127

ILIA *(da sé)*

Io tremo.

ELETTRA *(da sé)*

Io te'l direi.

IDOMENEO

Figlio, contro di me Nettuno irato
gelommi il cor; ogni tua tenerezza
l'affanno mio raddoppia, il tuo dolore
tutto sul cor mi piomba, e rimirarti
senza ribrezzo e orror non posso.

ILIA *(da sé)*

Oh Dio!

IDAMANTE

Forse per colpa mia Nettun sdegnossi;
ma la colpa qual è?

IDOMENEO

Ah, placarlo potessi
senza di te!

ELETTRA *(da sé)*

Ah potessi i torti miei
or vendicar!

IDOMENEO *(a Idamante)*

Parti, te lo comando,
fuggi il paterno lido e cerca altrove
sicuro asilo.

ILIA

Ahimè!...
(a Elettra) Pietosa principessa, ah mi conforta!

ELETTRA

Ch'io ti conforti? E come? *(da sé)* Ancor m'insulta
l'indegna.

IDAMANTE

Dunque io me n'andrò... ma dove?...
Oh Ilia!... oh genitor!

ILIA *(aside)*
> I tremble.

ELETTRA *(aside)*
> I could tell you.

IDOMENEO
My son, against my will, angry Neptune
has frozen my heart; your tenderness
redoubles my affliction, your sorrow
weighs on my heart, and I cannot look on you
without repugnance and horror.

ILIA *(aside)*
> Oh God!

IDAMANTE
Perhaps it is my fault that Neptune is angry?
But what is my crime?

IDOMENEO
Ah, if only I could appease him
without you!

ELETTRA *(aside)*
> Ah, if only I could
avenge my wrongs now!

IDOMENEO *(to Idamante)*
> Go, I command you:
fly your native shore and seek
safe refuge elsewhere.

ILIA
> Alas!
(to Elettra) Compassionate princess, comfort me!

ELETTRA
I, comfort you? How so? *(aside)* The shameless woman
insults me again.

IDAMANTE
> Then I will go... But where?
Oh Ilia! Oh, my father!

ILIA *(risoluta)*
O seguirti o morir, mio ben, vogl'io.

IDAMANTE
Deh resta, oh cara, e vivi in pace... Addio!

N°21 *Quartetto*

IDAMANTE
Andrò ramingo e solo,   [21]
morte cercando altrove
fin che la incontrerò.

ILIA
M'avrai compagna al duolo,
dove sarai, e dove
tu moia, io morirò.

IDAMANTE
Ah no...

IDOMENEO
Nettun spietato!
Chi per pietà m'uccide?

ELETTRA *(da sé)*
Quando vendetta avrò?

IDAMANTE, ILIA *(a due)*
(a Idomeneo)
Serena il ciglio irato.

ILIA, IDAMANTE, IDOMENEO *(a tre)*
Ah il cor mi si divide!

ILIA, ELETTRA, IDAMANTE, IDOMENEO *(a quattro)*
Soffrir più non si può.
Peggio è di morte
sì gran dolore.
più fiera sorte,
pena maggiore
nissun provò!

ILIA *(resolutely)*
  I desire to follow you or die, my beloved.

IDAMANTE
  Ah, stay here, dearest, and live in peace. Farewell!

No. 21 Quartet

IDAMANTE
  I will go wandering alone,   [21]
    seeking death elsewhere
    until I find it.

ILIA
  You will have me as your companion in sorrow
    wherever you are; and where
    you die, I too will die.

IDAMANTE
  Ah no!

IDOMENEO
      Pitiless Neptune!
  Who will kill me, for mercy's sake?

ELETTRA *(aside)*
  When will I be revenged?

IDAMANTE, ILIA *(together)*
(to Idomeneo)
  Calm your angry brow.

ILIA, IDAMANTE, IDOMENEO *(together)*
  Ah, my heart is breaking!

ILIA, ELETTRA, IDAMANTE, IDOMENEO *(together)*
  It is impossible to suffer more.
    Such great grief
    is worse than death.
    No one ever suffered
    a harsher fate,
    or greater pain!

131

IDAMANTE
Andrò ramingo e solo.

(parte addolorato)

Scena IV

Arbace, Idomeneo, Ilia, Elettra

ARBACE
Sire, alla reggia tua immensa turba
di popolo affollato ad alta voce
parlarti chiede.

ILIA *(da sé)*
A qualche nuovo affanno
preparati, mio cor.

IDOMENEO *(da sé)*
Perduto è il figlio.

ARBACE
Del Dio de' mari il sommo sacerdote
la guida.

IDOMENEO *(da sé)*
Ahi troppo disperato è il caso!...
Intesi, Arbace.

ELETTRA
Qual nuovo disastro?

ILIA
Il popol sollevato?...

IDOMENEO
Or vado ad ascoltarla. *(parte confuso)*

ELETTRA
Ti seguirò! *(parte)*

ILIA
Voglio seguirti anch'io. *(parte)*

132

IDAMANTE
    I will go wandering alone.

(exit sorrowfully)

Scene IV

Arbace, Idomeneo, Ilia, Elettra

ARBACE
    Sire, an immense crowd of people
    is thronging before your palace, and clamouring
    for you to speak.

ILIA *(aside)*
                    My heart, prepare yourself
    for some new affliction.

IDOMENEO *(aside)*
                    My son is lost.

ARBACE
    The high priest of the sea god
    leads the crowd.

IDOMENEO *(aside)*
    (Ah, the situation is desperate!)
    I understand, Arbace.

ELETTRA
    What new disaster?

ILIA
    Are the people rebelling?

IDOMENEO
    I go now to hear them. *(exit, confused)*

ELETTRA
    I will follow you! *(exit)*

ILIA
                    I too will follow you. *(exit)*

Scena V

Arbace solo

ARBACE

Sventurata Sidon! In te quai miro   [22a]
di morte, stragi e orror lugubri aspetti?
Ah Sidon più non sei,
sei la città del pianto, e questa reggia
quella del duol!... Dunque è per noi dal cielo
sbandita ogni pietà?...
Chi sa? Io spero ancora
che qualche nume amico
si plachi a tanto sangue; un nume solo
basta tutti a piegar; alla clemenza   [22b]
il rigor cederà... Ma ancor non scorgo
qual ci miri pietoso... Ah sordo è il cielo!
Ah Creta tutta io vedo
finir sua gloria sotto alte rovine!
No, sue miserie pria non avran fine.

N°22 Aria

Se colà ne' fati è scritto,   [22c]
    Creta, oh Dei, s'è rea, or cada,
    paghi il fio del suo delitto;
    ma salvate il prence, il re.
Deh d'un sol vi plachi il sangue!
    Ecco il mio, se il mio v'aggrada,
    e il bel regno, che già langue,
    giusti Dei! abbia mercé.

(parte)

Scena VI

Gran piazza abbellita di statue avanti al palazzo, di cui si vede da un lato il frontispicio. [23a]
Arriva Idomeneo accompagnato d'Arbace e del seguito reale; il re scortato d'Arbace si siede sopra il trono destinato alle pubbliche udienze; Gran Sacerdote e quantità di popolo. [23b]

134

Scene V

Arbace alone

ARBACE

    Unhappy Cydonia! What gloomy scenes   [22a]
    of death, slaughter and horror do I see in you!
    Ah, you are no longer Cydonia,
    you are the city of tears, and this palace
    that of sorrow!... Then does Heaven
    deny us all pity?
    Who knows? I still hope
    that some kindly god
    will be satisfied with all this blood; one single god
    is enough to make all the gods give way; severity   [22b]
    will yield to clemency... But I do not yet discern
    who might look pityingly on us. Heaven is deaf!
    Ah, I see all of Crete
    end her glory beneath a mass of ruins!
    No, her woes will not be over until then.

No. 22 Aria

    If thus it is written in the fates,   [22c]
      O gods, let Crete fall, if she is guilty,
      let her pay the penalty for her crime;
      but save the prince, the king.
    Ah, let the blood of a single man placate you!
      Here is mine, if mine will content you,
      and on this fair kingdom, which now languishes,
      have mercy, just gods!

(exit)

Scene VI

A great square adorned with statues in front of the palace, the façade of which is seen to one side. [23a]
Idomeneo arrives, accompanied by Arbace and the royal retinue; the king, escorted by Arbace, sits on the throne used for public audiences; the High Priest and a crowd of people. [23b]

135

N°23 *Recitativo*

GRAN SACERDOTE
 Volgi intorno lo sguardo, oh sire, e vedi
 qual strage orrenda nel tuo nobil regno
 fa il crudo mostro. Ah mira
 allagate di sangue
 quelle pubbliche vie; ad ogni passo
 vedrai chi geme e l'alma
 gonfia d'atro velen dal corpo esala.
 Mille e mille, in quell'ampio e sozzo ventre,
 pria sepolti che morti
 perire io stesso vidi.
 Sempre di sangue lorde
 son quelle fauci, e son sempre più ingorde.
 Da te solo dipende
 il ripiego, da morte trar tu puoi
 il resto del tuo popolo, ch'esclama
 sbigottito, e da te l'aiuto implora,
 e indugi ancor?... Al tempio, sire, al tempio.
 Qual è, dov'è la vittima?... a Nettuno
 rendi quello ch'è suo...

IDOMENEO
 Non più. Sacro ministro,
 e voi popoli, udite:
 la vittima è Idamante, e or or vedrete,   [23c]
 ah Numi! con qual ciglio?
 svenar il genitor il proprio figlio. *(parte turbato)*

N°24 *Coro*

CORO
 Oh voto tremendo!   [24a]
  Spettacolo orrendo!
  Già regna la morte,
  d'abisso le porte
  spalanca crudel.

GRAN SACERDOTE
 Oh cielo clemente!
  Il figlio è innocente,

No. 23 Recitative

HIGH PRIEST

Look around you, sire, and see
the horrible carnage wreaked in your noble realm
by this cruel monster. Ah, behold
the pools of blood
in the public thoroughfares; at each step
you will see someone groaning and giving up the ghost
from a body swollen with black poison.
I myself have seen thousands upon thousands perish,
swallowed up even before they are dead
in that vast foul belly.
Its jaws are always stained with blood
and ever greedier.
On you alone depends
the remedy. You can save from death
the rest of your people, who cry out
in dismay and implore your help; yet still
you delay? To the temple, sire, to the temple!
Who and where is the victim? Render to Neptune
that which is his...

IDOMENEO

No more. Sacred minister,
and you, my people, listen:
the victim is Idamante, and now you will see   [23c]
(ye gods, with what a countenance?)
a father sacrificing his own son. *(exit, distressed)*

No. 24 Chorus

CHORUS

Oh terrible vow!   [24a]
    Horrendous sight!
    Already death reigns,
    and cruelly throws opens
    the gates of the abyss.

HIGH PRIEST

O merciful Heaven!
    The son is innocent,

137

il voto è inumano;
arresta la mano
del padre fedel.

CORO
Oh voto tremendo!
Spettacolo orrendo!
Già regna la morte,
d'abisso le porte
spalanca crudel. *(partono tutti dolenti)* [24b]

Scena VII

Veduta esteriore del magnifico tempio di Nettuno con vastissimo atrio che lo circonda, a traverso del quale si scuopre in lontano spiaggia di mare.
L'atrio e le gallerie del tempio sono ripiene d'una moltitudine di popolo, i sacerdoti preparano le cose appartenenti al sacrificio.

N°25 *Marcia* [25]

Arriva Idomeneo accompagnato di numeroso e fastoso seguito.

N°26 *Cavatina con coro*

IDOMENEO
Accogli, oh re del mar, i nostri voti, [26]
placa lo sdegno tuo, il tuo rigor!

SACERDOTI
Accogli, oh re del mar, i nostri voti,
placa lo sdegno tuo, il tuo rigor!

IDOMENEO
Tornino a lor spelonche gl'Euri, i Noti,
torni Zeffiro al mar, cessi il furor!
Il pentimento e il cor de' tuoi divoti
accetta, e a noi concedi il tuo favor.

IDOMENEO E SACERDOTI
Accogli, oh re del mar, i nostri voti,
placa lo sdegno tuo, il tuo rigor!

the vow is inhuman;
stay the hand
of this pious father.

CHORUS
Oh terrible vow!
Horrendous sight!
Already death reigns,
and cruelly throws opens
the gates of the abyss. *(exeunt omnes, grieving)*   [24b]

Scene VII

*The exterior of the magnificent temple of Neptune, surrounded
by a vast atrium, through which the seashore can be seen in the
distance.*
*The atrium and arcades of the temple are filled with a crowd of
people; the priests are making preparations for the sacrifice.*

No. 25 March   [25]

Idomeneo arrives, accompanied by a large and splendid retinue.

No. 26 Cavatina with chorus

IDOMENEO
Receive our vows, O king of the sea,   [26]
abate your anger, your severity!

PRIESTS
Receive our vows, O king of the sea,
abate your anger, your severity!

IDOMENEO
Let Eurus and Notus return to their caverns;
    let Zephyrus* return to the sea; let their fury cease!
Accept the repentance and the hearts
    of your devotees, and grant us your favour.

IDOMENEO AND PRIESTS
Receive our vows, O king of the sea,
    abate your anger, your severity!

CORO *(entro le scene)*
Stupenda vittoria!
Eterna è tua gloria,
trionfa, oh signor!

IDOMENEO
Qual risuona qui intorno
applauso di vittoria?

Scena VIII

Arbace frettoloso, e detti

ARBACE
Sire, il prence,
Idamante l'eroe, di morte in traccia
disperato correndo
il trionfo trovò. Su l'empio mostro
scagliossi furibondo, il vinse, e uccise.
Eccoci salvi alfin.

IDOMENEO
Ahimè! Nettuno
di nuovo sdegno acceso
sarà contro di noi… Or or, Arbace,
con tuo dolor vedrai
che Idamante trovò quel che cercava,
e di morte egli stesso
il trionfo sarà.

ARBACE *(vede condurre Idamante)*
Che vedo? oh Numi!

Scena IX

*Idamante in veste bianca con ghirlanda di fiori in capo, circon-
dato da guardie e da sacerdoti. Moltitudine di mesto popolo, e
suddetti.*

N°27 Recitativo e Aria

IDAMANTE
Padre, mio caro padre, ah dolce nome!   [27a]
Eccomi, a' piedi tuoi. In questo estremo

CHORUS *(offstage)*
Tremendous victory!
Eternal is your glory!
Triumph, O lord!

IDOMENEO
What are these shouts
of victory that echo around us?

Scene VIII

Arbace entering in haste, and the previous

ARBACE
Sire, Prince Idamante,
the hero, running desperately
to meet death,
has found triumph. He threw himself furiously
on the cruel monster, vanquished and killed it.
We are saved at last.

IDOMENEO
Alas! Neptune's anger
will again flare up
against us... Now, Arbace,
to your sorrow you will see
that Idamante has found what he was seeking,
and that it is death
that will triumph over him.

ARBACE *(seeing Idamante being led in)*
What do I see? Oh gods!

Scene IX

Idamante in a white robe, with a garland of flowers on his head, and surrounded by guards and priests. A multitude of sorrowing people, and the previous.

No. 27 Recitative and Aria

IDAMANTE
Father, my dear father! Ah, sweet name!   [27a]
Behold me at your feet. At this ultimate,

141

periodo fatal, su questa destra
che il varco al sangue tuo nelle mie vene
aprir dovrà, gl'ultimi baci accetta.
Ora comprendo che il tuo turbamento
sdegno non era già, ma amor paterno.
Oh mille volte e mille
fortunato Idamante,
se chi vita ti diè vita ti toglie,
e togliendola a te la rende al cielo,   [27b]
e dal cielo la sua in cambio impetra,
ed impetra costante a' suoi la pace
e de' Numi l'amor sacro e verace!

IDOMENEO
Oh figlio! oh caro figlio!...   [27c]
Perdona: il crudo uffizio
in me scelta non è, pena è del fato.
Barbaro, iniquo fato!... Ah no, non posso
contro un figlio innocente
alzar l'aspra bipenne... Da ogni fibra
già sen fuggon le forze, e gl'occhi miei
torbida notte ingombra... oh figlio!...

IDAMANTE (*languente, poi risoluto*)

                      Oh padre!...

Ah non t'arresti inutile pietà,
né vana ti lusinghi
tenerezza d'amor. Deh vibra un colpo
che ambi tolga d'affanno.

IDOMENEO
                 Ah che natura
mel contrasta e ripugna.

IDAMANTE
Ceda natura al suo autor: di Giove
questo è l'alto voler.
Rammenta il tuo dover. Se un figlio perdi,
cento avrai Numi amici. Figli tuoi
i tuoi popoli sono...

fatal moment, on that right hand
which must make your blood flow from my veins,
accept my last kisses.
Now I understand that your agitation
was not anger, but paternal love.
Oh, a thousand times fortunate
are you, Idamante,
if he who gave you life takes it from you,
and in taking it gives it to Heaven,   [27b]
to receive from Heaven his own in exchange
and thus obtain lasting peace for his people
and the sacred and true love of the gods!

IDOMENEO   [27c]
My son! My dear son!
Forgive me: this cruel task
is not my choice, but the punishment of fate:
barbarous, unjust fate!... Ah no, I cannot
raise the savage axe
against an innocent son... Strength ebbs
from every fibre of my body, and dark night
clouds my eyes... Oh, my son!

IDAMANTE *(stricken, then resolute)*
My father!
Do not let futile pity stay your hand,
nor the vain tenderness of love
beguile you. Come, strike the blow
that will relieve us both of our affliction.

IDOMENEO
Ah, nature
prevents me from doing so, and rebels against it.

IDAMANTE
Let nature yield to its creator: such is
the mighty will of Jupiter.
Remember your duty. If you lose a son,
you will gain a hundred friendly gods. Your people
are your children...

143

Ma se in mia vece brami
chi t'ubbidisca ed ami,
chi ti sia accanto e di tue cure il peso
teco ne porti... Ilia ti raccomando...
Deh un figlio tu esaudisci
che moribondo supplica e consiglia:
s'ella sposa non m'è, deh siati figlia.

No, la morte io non pavento,   [27d]
    se alla patria, al genitore
    frutta, o Numi, il vostro amore
    e di pace il bel seren.
Agli Elisi andrò contento,
    e riposo avrà quest'alma,
    se in lasciare la mia salma
    vita e pace avrà il mio ben.

Ma che più tardi? Eccomi pronto, adempi
il sacrifizio, il voto.

IDOMENEO
                    Oh qual mi sento
in ogni vena insolito vigor?...
Or risoluto son... l'ultimo amplesso
ricevi... e mori.

IDAMANTE
                    Oh padre!...

IDOMENEO
                            Oh figlio!...

IDAMANTE, IDOMENEO *(a due)*
                                Oh Dio!...

IDAMANTE *(da sé)*
    Oh Ilia... ahimè!... *(a Idomeneo)* Vivi felice.

IDOMENEO e IDAMANTE *(a due)*
                                Addio!

But if you wish someone in my place
to obey and love you,
who will be by your side and bear with you
the burden of your cares, I commend Ilia to you.
Ah, grant the wish of a son
who beseeches and counsels you as he dies:
if she is not my wife, let her be your daughter.

No, I do not fear death, [27d]
  if your love, O gods, brings
  my country and my father
  the sweet serenity of peace.
I will gladly go to the Elysian Fields,
  and my soul will be at rest,
  if I know, as I quit my mortal flesh,
  that my beloved will have life and peace.

But why do you delay? See, I am ready: perform
the sacrifice, fulfil your vow.

IDOMENEO

                        Ah, what is this unwonted strength
I feel in every vein?
Now I am resolved. Receive
my last embrace... and die.

IDAMANTE

               My father!

IDOMENEO

                 My son!

IDAMANTE, IDOMENEO *(together)*

                       Oh God!

IDAMANTE *(aside)*
  Oh, Ilia... Alas! *(to Idomeneo)* Be happy.

IDOMENEO and IDAMANTE *(together)*

                   Farewell!

Scena X

Ilia frettolosa, Elettra, e detti

ILIA *(corre a ritenere il braccio d'Idomeneo)*
  Ferma, oh sire, che fai?

IDOMENEO
  La vittima io sveno
  che promisi a Nettuno.

IDAMANTE
                    Ilia, t'accheta.

GRAN SACERDOTE *(a Ilia)*
  Deh non turbar il sacrifizio.

ILIA
                    Invano
  quella scure altro petto
  tenta ferir. Eccoti, sire, il mio,
  la vittima io son.

ELETTRA *(da sé)*
                    Oh qual contrasto!

ILIA *(a Idomeneo)*
  Innocente è Idamante, è figlio tuo,
  e del regno è la speme.
  Tiranni i Dei non son. Fallaci siete
  interpreti voi tutti
  del divino voler. Vuol sgombra il cielo
  de' nemici la Grecia, e non de' figli.
  Benché innocente anch'io, benché ora amica,
  di Priamo son figlia, e Frigia io nacqui,
  per natura nemica al greco nome.
  Orsù, mi svena…

IDAMANTE
                    Ah troppo,
  Ilia, sei generosa;
  vittima sì preziosa il genitore
  non promise a Nettun, me scelse il fato.

146

Scene X

Ilia in haste, Elettra, the previous

ILIA *(running to restrain Idomeneo's arm)*
Stop, sire, what are you doing?

IDOMENEO
I must slay the victim
whom I promised to Neptune.

IDAMANTE
                    Ilia, be calm.

HIGH PRIEST *(to Ilia)*
Do not disturb the sacrifice.

ILIA
                    In vain
that axe seeks to wound
another breast. Here is mine, sire:
I am the victim.

ELETTRA *(aside)*
            Oh, what a reversal of fortune!

ILIA *(to Idomeneo)*
Idamante is innocent; he is your son,
and the hope of the kingdom.
The gods are not tyrants. You are all
false interpreters
of the divine will. Heaven wishes to rid Greece
of her enemies, not of her sons.
Although I am innocent, and now your friend,
I am Priam's daughter, and was born a Phrygian,
by nature an enemy to the name of Greece.
Come now, kill me…

IDAMANTE
            Ah, Ilia,
you are too generous;
my father did not promise Neptune
so precious a victim. It is I who was chosen by fate.

La Frigia in te ancor vive:
chi sa a qual fine il ciel ti serba in vita,
e della Grecia in sen?

ILIA

      Invan m'alletti.

IDAMANTE

Invan morir presumi.

IDOMENEO

Ah ch'io son fuor di me. Soccorso, oh Numi!

ARBACE

Oh ciel! che fia?… mi scoppia il cor…

ELETTRA *(da sé)*

         In petto
quai moti ardenti io sento
di rabbia e di furor!

GRAN SACERDOTE

Sire, risolvi omai.

ILIA

     Eccomi all'ara.

IDOMENEO

Ma quella tu non sei…

ILIA

Sempre più grata è ai Dei
vittima volontaria.

IDAMANTE

     Idolo mio!
Deh dàmmi del tuo amor l'ultimo pegno.

ILIA

Ecco il mio sangue.

IDAMANTE

     Ah no. La gloria in pace
lasciami di morire
per la mia patria.

Phrygia lives on in you:
who knows to what end Heaven preserves your life
in the very bosom of Greece?

ILIA

In vain you try to sway me.

IDAMANTE
In vain you profess to die.

IDOMENEO
Ah, I can bear no more. Help me, O gods!

ARBACE
Oh Heaven, what is to happen? My heart is bursting...

ELETTRA *(aside)*

What

burning emotions of rage and fury
I feel in my breast!

HIGH PRIEST
Sire, you must decide now.

ILIA

Behold, I am on the altar.

IDOMENEO
But you are not the one...

ILIA
A willing victim
is always more welcome to the gods.

IDAMANTE

My idol!

Ah, give me a last pledge of your love.

ILIA
Here is my blood.

IDAMANTE

Ah no: leave me the glory

of dying in peace
for my country.

ILIA

A me s'aspetta.

IDAMANTE

Oh Dio!

ILIA

Gratitudine è in me.

IDAMANTE

In me è dover.

ILIA

Ma ti dispensa amore.
Nettun! Eccoti il cambio

(Corre all'ara; vuole inginocchiarsi; Idamante la ritiene.)

IDAMANTE

O vivi o parti, o insiem noi moriremo.

ILIA

No, sola io vuo' varcar il guado estremo.
A te, sacro ministro…

(S'inginocchia avanti al Gran Sacerdote. Nell'atto stesso che Ilia s'inginocchia, s'ode un gran strepito sotterraneo. Il simolacro di Nettuno si scuote, il Gran Sacerdote si trova avanti l'ara in estasi. Tutti rimangono attoniti ed immobili per lo spavento. Una voce profonda pronunzia la seguente sentenza del cielo.)

N°28

LA VOCE

Ha vinto amore…   [28]
A Idomeneo perdona
il gran trascorso il ciel… ma non al re,
a cui mancar non lice a sue promesse…
Cessi esser re… lo sia Idamante… ed Ilia
a lui sia sposa, e fia pago Nettuno,
contento il ciel, premiata l'innocenza.
La pace renderà di Creta al regno.
Stabilito nel ciel nodo sì degno.

ILIA

It is expected of me...

IDAMANTE

Oh God!

ILIA

It is gratitude in me.

IDAMANTE

It is my duty...

ILIA

But love dispenses you from it.
Neptune! Here I am in exchange!

(She runs to the altar and tries to kneel; Idamante holds her back.)

IDAMANTE

Either live, and leave now, or we die together.

ILIA

No, I want to cross the last ford alone.
Now, sacred minister...

(She kneels before the High Priest. As she does so, a great commotion is heard underground. The statue of Neptune moves; the High Priest stands in ecstasy before the altar. All remained stunned and motionless with fear. A deep voice pronounces the sentence of Heaven.)

No. 28

THE VOICE

Love has conquered...   [28]

Heaven pardons Idomeneo
for his great fault... but not as king,
for a king may not renounce his promises.
Let him cease to reign, and Idamante take his place
with Ilia as his wife. Thus Neptune will be appeased,
Heaven contented, and innocence rewarded.
He will restore peace to the kingdom of Crete.
So worthy a marriage was arranged in Heaven.

IDOMENEO

Oh ciel pietoso!

IDAMANTE

Ilia...

ILIA

Idamante, udisti?

ARBACE

Oh gioia! oh amor! oh Numi!

ELETTRA

Oh smania! oh furie! oh disperata Elettra!
Addio amor, addio speme! Ah il cor nel seno
già m'ardono l'Eumenidi spietate.
Misera, a che m'arresto?
Sarò in queste contrade
della gioia e trionfi
spettatrice dolente?
Vedrò Idamante alla rivale in braccio,
e dall'uno e dall'altra
mostrarmi a dito? Ah no, il germano Oreste
ne' cupi abissi io vuo'
seguir. Ombra infelice!
Lo spirito mio accogli, or or compagna
m'avrai là nell'inferno
a sempiterni guai, al pianto eterno.

N°29 Aria

D'Oreste, d'Aiace   [29]
 ho in seno i tormenti.
 D'Aletto la face
 già morte mi dà.
Squarciatemi il core,
 ceraste, serpenti,
 o un ferro il dolore
 in me finirà.

(parte infuriata)

IDOMENEO
    Oh merciful Heaven!

IDAMANTE
                        Ilia...

ILIA
                            Idamante, did you hear?

ARBACE
    Oh joy! Oh love! Oh gods!

ELETTRA
    Oh rage! Oh furies! Oh despairing Elettra!
    Farewell love, farewell hope! Ah, the merciless
    Eumenides* already scorch my heart in my bosom.
    Wretch that I am, why do I delay?
    Shall I remain in this land
    as a sorrowing witness
    to joy and triumphs?
    Shall I see Idamante in my rival's arms,
    and have every finger
    pointed at me? Ah no, I want to follow
    my brother Orestes into the deep abyss.
    Unhappy shade,
    receive my spirit! Now you will have me
    as your companion in hell,
    amid eternal woes and everlasting tears.

No. 29 Aria

    Within my breast I feel   [29]
        the torments of Orestes and Ajax.*
        Alecto's* torch
        now brings me death.
    Tear out my heart,
        horned vipers, serpents,
        or else a blade will put an end
        to my pain.

(exit, wild with fury)

153

Scena ultima

*Idomeneo, Idamante, Ilia, Arbace. Seguito d'Idomeneo, d'Idamante
e d'Ilia; popolo*   [30a]

IDOMENEO

Popoli, a voi l'ultima legge impone
Idomeneo qual re. Pace v'annunzio,
compiuto è il sacrifizio, e sciolto il voto.
Nettuno e tutti i Numi a questo regno
amici son. Resta che al cenno loro
Idomeneo ora ubbidisca. Oh quanto,
o sommi Dei, quanto m'è grato il cenno!
Eccovi un altro re, un altro me stesso.
A Idamante mio figlio, al caro figlio
cedo il soglio di Creta e tutto insieme
il sovrano poter. I suoi comandi
rispettate, eseguite ubbidienti,
come i miei eseguiste e rispettaste;
onde grato io vi son: questa è la legge.
Eccovi la real sposa. Mirate
in questa bella coppia un don del cielo
serbato a voi. Quanto a sperar vi lice!
Oh Creta fortunata; oh me felice!

N°30a *Aria*

Torna la pace al core   [30b]
    torna lo spento ardore;
    fiorisce in me l'età.
Tal la stagion di Flora
    l'albero annoso infiora,
    nuovo vigor gli dà.

*(Segue l'incoronazione d'Idamante, che s'eseguisce in pantomima,
ed il coro, che si canta durante l'incoronazione, ed il ballo.)*

N°31 *Coro*

Scenda Amor, scenda Imeneo,   [31]
    e Giunone ai regi sposi.
    D'alma pace omai li posi
    la Dea pronuba nel sen.

N°32 *Ballet*   [32]

Final Scene

Idomeneo, Idamante, Ilia, Arbace. Retinues of Idomeneo, Idamante, and Ilia; the people   [30a]

IDOMENEO
My people, Idomeneo imposes on you his final law
as king. I proclaim peace.
The sacrifice is fulfilled; I am released from my vow.
Neptune and all the gods look kindly
on this kingdom. It remains only for Idomeneo
to do their bidding. O mighty gods,
how dear your command is to me!
Here is another king for you, my other self.
To my son Idamante, my dear son,
I relinquish the throne of Crete, and with it
my sovereign power. Respect
his commands, follow them obediently,
as you have followed and respected mine,
for which I am grateful. That is my law.
Here is the royal bride. Behold
in this handsome couple a gift bestowed on you
by Heaven. What hopes may now be yours!
O fortunate Crete! How happy I am!

No. 30 Aria

Peace returns to my heart,   [30b]
    my spent ardour is reborn,
    and youth blooms anew in me.
Thus does the season of Flora*
    deck the aged tree with blossom
    and give it renewed vigour.

(There follow the coronation of Idamante, performed in mime, and the chorus, which is sung during the coronation, then the ballet.)

No. 31 Chorus

Let Love, and Hymen,   [31]
    and Juno descend on the royal pair.
    May the goddess of marriage
    fill their breasts with peace.

No. 32 Ballet   [32]

Notes

p. 65, *Orestes*: Elettra's brother; he has killed their mother Clytem-nestra and the latter's lover Aegisthus, who had previously mur-dered the pair's father Agamemnon, king of Mycenae (Argos), on his return from the Trojan War.

p. 67, *Ilium*: another name for Troy (hence Ilia's own name).

p. 67, *Cytherea's son*: Cupid (Love), son of Venus (Cytherea).

p. 69, *Cydonia*: ancient Kydonia (not Sidon in Phoenicia), on the site of the modern town of Chaniá, which Varesco seems to have thought of as the capital of Crete rather than Knossos.

p. 75, *Avernus*: the Underworld.

p. 79, *blond god*: Apollo

p. 91, *Portunus*: a sea god, protector of havens (Palaemon in Greek).

p. 91, *Amphitrite*: Neptune's consort.

p. 91, *Dis*: also known as Pluto (or Hades in Greek), god of the Underworld.

p. 93, *Aeolus*: ruler of the winds.

p. 101, *god of Delos*: Apollo.

p. 101, *grey-eyed goddess*: Minerva (Athena Glaucopis in Greek).

p. 111, *Boreas*: the north wind.

p. 137, *Eurus… Notus… Zephyrus*: respectively the east, south and west winds.

p. 151, *Eumenides*: the Furies or Erinyes, who wreak divine venge-ance on wrong-doers.

p. 151, *torments of Orestes and Ajax*: Orestes went mad after kill-ing his mother, as did the Greek commander Ajax after he was refused the arms of the dead Achilles.

p. 151, *Alecto's*: Alecto, one of the Furies, represented armed with flaming torches, her head covered with serpents.

p. 153, *Flora*: goddess of flowering plants, and thus of the season of spring.

Select Discography

There are two principal versions of *Idomeneo*, one written for Munich in 1781 and one for Vienna in 1786. For Vienna, Mozart made substantial cuts, wrote two new numbers and rewrote the castrato role of Idamante for a tenor. For the Munich performances, Mozart also made substantial alterations to what he had composed, especially in the last act. The available recordings of the opera reflect the lack of any definitive performing edition.

For detailed information and comparisons, see William Mann, '*Idomeneo* and *La Clemenza di Tito*', *Opera on Record*, ed. Alan Blyth (London: Hutchinson, 1979), pp. 42–50 and David Hamilton, '*Idomeneo, Rè di Creta*' (1781)', *The Metropolitan Opera Guide to Recorded Opera*, ed. Paul Gruber (New York and London: Thames & Hudson, 1993), pp. 272–77.

YEAR	CAST (IDOMENEO IDAMANTE ILIA ELETTRA)	CONDUCTOR/ORCHESTRA	LABEL
1951	Richard Lewis Léopold Simoneau Sena Jurinac Birgit Nilsson	Fritz Busch Glyndebourne Festival	Symposium (excerpts)
1956	Richard Lewis Léopold Simoneau Sena Jurinac Lucille Udovick	John Pritchard Glyndebourne Festival	EMI Références

1968	George Shirley Ryland Davies Margherita Rinaldi Pauline Tinsley	Colin Davis BBC Symphony	Philips
1972	Nicolai Gedda Adolf Dallapozza Anneliese Rothenberger Edda Moser	Hans Schmidt-Isserstedt Dresden Staatskapelle	EMI Classics
1977	Wiesław Ochman Peter Schreier Edith Mathis Julia Varady	Karl Böhm Dresden Staatskapelle	DG
1980	Werner Hollweg Trudeliese Schmidt Rachel Yakar Felicity Palmer	Nikolaus Harnoncourt Zurich Opera House	Teldec
1983	Luciano Pavarotti Agnes Baltsa Lucia Popp Edita Gruberová	John Pritchard Vienna Philharmonic	Decca
1990	Anthony Rolfe Johnson Anne Sofie von Otter Sylvia McNair Hillevi Martinpelto	John Eliot Gardiner English Baroque Soloists	Archiv
1991	Francisco Araiza Susanne Mentzer Barbara Hendricks Roberta Alexander	Colin Davis Bavarian Radio	Philips
1994	Plácido Domingo Cecilia Bartoli Heidi Grant Murphy Carol Vaness	James Levine Metropolitan Opera	DG

2002	Ian Bostridge Lorraine Hunt Lieberson Lisa Milne Barbara Frittoli	Charles Mackerras Scottish Chamber	EMI Classics
2004	Bruce Ford Diana Montague Rebecca Evans Susan Patterson	David Parry Opera North	Chandos (sung in English)
2007	Robert Gambill Iris Vermillion Britta Stallmeister Camilla Nylund	Fabio Luisi Dresden Staatskapelle	Orfeo d'Or (Strauss version)
2009	Richard Croft Bernarda Fink Sunhae Im Alexandrina Pendatchanska	René Jacobs Freiburger Barockorchester	Harmonia Mundi

Idomeneo on DVD

For more detailed listing, see Ken Wlaschin, *Encyclopedia of Opera on Screen* (Yale: Yale University Press, 2004)

YEAR	CAST (IDOMENEO IDAMANTE ILIA ELETTRA)	CONDUCTOR	DIRECTOR/COMPANY
1969	Peter Pears Anne Pashley Heather Harper Rae Woodland	Benjamin Britten	Colin Graham English Opera Group
1974	Richard Lewis Leo Goeke Bozena Betley Josephine Barstow	John Pritchard	John Cox Glyndebourne Festival
1982	Luciano Pavarotti Frederica von Stade Ileana Cotrubas Hildegard Behrens	James Levine	Jean-Pierre Ponnelle Metropolitan Opera
1983	Philip Langridge Jerry Hadley Yvonne Kenny Carol Vaness	Bernard Haitink	Trevor Nunn Glyndebourne Festival
1991	Stuart Kale David Kuebler Ann Christine Biel Anita Soldh	Arnold Östman	Michael Hampe Drottningholm

2004	Kurt Streit Sonia Ganassi Ángeles Blancas Gulin Iano Tamar	Marco Guidarini	Pier Luigi Pizzi Teatro San Carlo di Napoli
2006	Ramón Vargas Magdalena Kožená Ekaterina Siurina Anja Harteros	Roger Norrington	Ursel and Karl- Ernst Herrmann Salzburg Festival
2008	John Mark Ainsley Pavol Breslik Juliane Banse Annette Dasch	Kent Nagano	Dieter Dorn Bayerische Staatsoper
2008	Saimir Pirgu Marie-Claude Chappuis Julia Kleiter Eva Mei	Nikolaus Harnoncourt	Nikolaus and Philipp Harnoncourt Styriarte Festival, Graz

Select Bibliography

Angermüller, Rudolph. *Mozart's Operas*, trans. Stewart Spencer (New York: Rizzoli International, 1988)

Cairns, David. *Mozart and His Operas* (London: Allen Lane, 2006)

Eisen, Cliff and Keefe, Simon P. (eds.). *The Cambridge Mozart Encyclopedia* (Cambridge: Cambridge University Press, 2006)

Eisen, Cliff (ed.). *Mozart: A Life in Letters*, trans. Stewart Spencer (London: Penguin, 2006)

Gutman, Robert W. *Mozart: A Cultural Biography* (New York: Harcourt Brace & Co., 1999)

Heartz, Daniel (ed.). *Mozart's Operas* (Berkeley: University of California Press, 1990)

Hunter, Mary. *Mozart's Operas: A Companion* (New Haven: Yale University Press, 2008)

Keefe, Simon P. (ed.). *The Cambridge Companion to Mozart* (Cambridge: Cambridge University Press, 2003)

Landon, H. C. Robbins (ed.). *The Mozart Compendium* (London: Thames & Hudson, 1990)

Landon, H. C. Robbins and Donald Mitchell (eds.). *The Mozart Companion* (London: Rockliff, 1956)

Mann, William. *The Operas of Mozart* (London: Cassell, 1977)

Rushton, Julian. *W. A. Mozart: Idomeneo* (Cambridge: Cambridge University Press, 1993)

Sadie, Stanley (ed.). *Wolfgang Amadè Mozart* (Oxford: Clarendon Press, 1996)

Sadie, Stanley. *Mozart: The Early Years* (Oxford: Oxford University Press, 2006)

Till, Nicholas. *Mozart and the Enlightenment: Truth, Virtue and Beauty in Mozart's Operas* (London: Faber and Faber, 1992)

Mozart Websites

In English or with an English-language option

Apropos Mozart: www.aproposmozart.com

Associazione Mozart Italia: www.mozartitalia.org

Bärenreiter Mozart Portal: www.mozart-portal.de

British Library Online Gallery – Mozart's Thematic Catalogue (scroll down the page and click on 'Mozart's Musical Diary'): www.bl.uk/onlinegallery/ttp/ttpbooks.html

International Mozart Foundation: www.mozarteum.at

The Mozart Forum: www.mozartforum.com

The Mozart Project: www.mozartproject.org

Neue Mozart-Ausgabe Online: www.nma.at

Openmozart.net: www.openmozart.net

OperaGlass Mozart: opera.stanford.edu/Mozart

Salzburg Festival: www.salzburgfestival.com

Note on the Contributors

Nicholas Till is a historian, critic and theatre artist. He is the author of *Mozart and the Enlightenment* and is currently Professor of Opera and Music Theatre at the University of Sussex.

Julian Rushton, Emeritus Professor of Music at the University of Leeds, has published extensively on Mozart including *The New Grove Guide to Mozart's Operas* and the Cambridge Opera Handbook on *Idomeneo*.

Gary Kahn studied at Trinity College, Oxford. He has worked for BBC Television and English National Opera. His book *The Power of the Ring* was published by the Royal Opera House in 2007.

Charles Johnston studied languages and history at Glasgow and Oxford, then held several posts with French record companies. He is now a freelance translator and writer based in Strasbourg.

Acknowledgements

We would like to thank John Allison of *Opera* magazine and David Robson for their assistance and advice in the preparation of this Guide.

www.overturepublishing.com
www.eno.org